T0130016

I hope you will enjoy these two FREE gifts to help you in your life's journey

Please click the links below to access your gifts.

Relaxing Meditation (Instant download). Quote MEDCD16 in the coupon. http:/beingnaturallyhealthy.com/shop-cart/products-page/checkout/

E-book: *Vibrant Health and Vitality at any Age*
http:/beingnaturallyhealthy.com/shop-cart/free-ebook/

With Love and Blessings

Lessons
from Your Last Life

and How They Can Help You In This One

Diana Scanlan

BALBOA
PRESS

A DIVISION OF HAY HOUSE

Balboa Press books may be ordered through booksellers or by contacting:

Balboa Press
A Division of Hay House
1663 Liberty Drive
Bloomington, IN 47403
www.balboapress.com.au
1 (877) 407-4847

Print information available on the last page.

ISBN: 978-1-5043-0472-6 (sc)
ISBN: 978-1-5043-0473-3 (e)

Balboa Press rev. date: 10/12/2016

Contents

$\mathcal{I}$ntroduction

This is the true story of my escape from a challenging childhood and marital abuse to happiness. An epic journey across the world to a new continent where I met my soulmate and life partner. Ultimately finding my life purpose and receiving valuable insights to help others move through their life's journey.

Throughout this life, I have felt a strong connection with American Native Indians. In fact, as a child, I was obsessed with their culture, their spirituality and their connection with the Universe and the Earth. This feeling of connection, rather than subsiding, has increased throughout the years. I began to receive messages, insights, and lessons that I have carried from that life into this one. The trials I have endured and the gifts I have been blessed with have culminated in a powerful intuition to share this knowledge at this time of intense change.

This book, although written about my life, can be used to help you find insights in your own life. A chapter towards the end of the book is dedicated to insights and lessons. I have also shared my "Mountaintop Meditation" with you. It is my wish that with regular practice, this meditation will bring you happiness and serenity.

Love and light.

Diana

Acknowledgements

My deep gratitude to Hugh for his endless patience and suggestions and for transcribing my almost illegible handwriting. Also to my daughter Karen, for her support. Above all, I wish to thank my Divine who gave me the nudges and the inspiration to continue.

The journey begins

*Life in all its fullness and beauty, happiness and sorrows,
is given to us to evolve and to enrich the lives of others.*

Fear. Why is there so much fear? I hear my mother's heartbeat but all I sense from her is fear and resentment. Is it fear of the birthing process? No. There is something more. But what? And why this powerful resentment? Questions with no answers - yet. I curl up in her womb as if to protect myself but I know the time is drawing close when I must leave this warm, safe environment. Is my life's purpose to save humanity from themselves at this time when they are poised on the brink of self-destruction? No. Is it to awaken and enlighten them with love and inspiration? Why in this time of war and hatred? But of course, universal timing is never wrong. Humanity is hungry for this information.

Lessons from your past life can help you in this one. I came into this world kicking and screaming and very much aware of my mother's fear. Fear for her life and the life of her child. I hear bombs falling all around me and the noise is deafening, only muted by the sound of my cries. Until recently, this trauma has lingered with me through the years and I still have an aversion to loud noise. How badly I wanted to return to my previous life. There I had experienced peace, love, and support from my mother, father, and extended American Indian family. I remembered so vividly, the closeness of our small community and my strong connection to source, Spirit, God, and All That Is and to Mother Earth and Mother Nature.

With shock and disbelief, I instantly remembered how I left that life. At age twelve, I had developed peritonitis. The shaman had tried in vain to heal and save me, casting spells and using herbal poultices on my pain-ridden body. I remembered how his eyes met mine and conveyed intuitively that I would ultimately reach my potential as a healer and sage, but not in that life. At times, my past life as an American Indian child has been more real than this one. I see my mother standing above me. Her culture had created too strong a woman to show her grief at my impending death. I see my happy childhood, where I learnt to live with this simple, yet profound culture. I remember how my mother stood over me as I left and how I felt her love so strongly, little knowing that I would meet her again in my next life - this one.

Although my childhood home in this life was a few miles from the city, it was targeted because of its industrial centre and weapon-making factories. There were two bombings that narrowly missed our little row of houses. On the first occasion, I was sleeping with mum under the stairs (as she did every night, especially when my father was working night shifts). I woke with a start at the horrific sound. I felt the house shake and the sensation of being held in a tight grip. It almost took my breath away. I felt my mother's heart beating wildly and heard both our cries of fear. The huge hole, barely more than a few hundred yards away, was an irresistible magnet. As a young child, I was drawn to its edges, even though I knew that I was forbidden to enter its mysterious depths. My father was frequently angry and violent. I hesitated to venture in, for fear of inviting his anger.

It was not until many years later that I was able to completely forgive my father for his behaviour towards my family. How light and free I felt after I had done so. It was like putting that chapter of my life behind me and finally having the freedom to move forward with joy and gratitude. In my meditations, I subsequently saw my father (who had long since passed on from this life). I clearly heard him say, "I'm sorry." In that moment, I watched a rare smile light up his face, and we both experienced healing and intense love, such as is seldom felt or understood.

I was blessed indeed in this life to have spent my childhood living in the English countryside. My memories consist of a love of, and connection with, Mother Earth and Mother Nature. Of playing in the fields, climbing trees and exploring the streams. When I was quite young, I began to be obsessed with what others called red Indians. I would gather feathers from the fields, tuck them into my headband and dance around a make-believe fire.

I loved recording finds from nature. A certain flower, or sighting a kestrel or an eagle. Even at that age, I felt an affinity with eagles which has persisted throughout my life. Many times, I have felt their presence. When I looked up, I would see one flying directly above me, and the experience was one of such joy. A mentor later encouraged me to be as an eagle, fly above the clouds and shake off the crows that harass me. Translation: Cast off the cares and worries of this life by your unceasing positivity and persistence.

$\mathcal{C}$hildhood

My Mother and I

*No matter what challenges the universe sends your way,
stay strong, for these are opportunities in
disguise, to learn and move forward.*

Even though I remember few light-hearted moments in my home as I grew, my mother was a continual source of inspiration. Her patience and protection were a source of wonder in my childhood. She was always there. What a restricted and isolated life she must have led. She was a steadfast lady who possessed inner strength beyond my childhood understanding. Her black hair and olive skin were inherited from our Indian subcontinent ancestry. Although not tall in her youth, she seemed to shrink as she aged, as though the burden of her difficult life had weighed her down.

Then came the end of the war. Flags of celebration appeared in all our neighbours' homes. I stood on our handkerchief-sized lawn and marvelled at them fluttering in the breeze. Shortly afterwards, my brother John was born. I saw mum's attention move away from me and felt a certain sense of isolation and envy. How could this tiny, red-faced bundle be the cause of this shift in her affection? My child's mind told me that to win back her favour, I needed to find gifts (of course, from our own garden). I proudly presented her with caterpillars, a butterfly chrysalis, and numerous small insects. Not surprisingly, none of these met with her approval. More the reverse, "Diana, take them outside! Don't bring them into the house", was her stern rebuke. Little did I know, she actually understood my motivation. She softened the words with a much-appreciated hug and read one of my favourite stories from The Wind in the Willows.

I have no recall of the long, wet days or storm-ravaged nights of an English winter. My memories are imbued with sunshine, black-berrying along the lanes and in the small woodlands which surrounded our home. It filled my senses with the fragrance of a summer day that is unique to this part of our beautiful planet. This was followed by the baking of apple and blackberry pies. Hours of jam making and bottling the precious fruit in readiness for the long winters ahead.

A tiny ball of fur of a kitten was my first pet. Well, I called her mine as I walked home carefully cradling her in my arms. I was six, and she was six weeks old, barely old enough to be taken from her mother and her siblings. She was loved and cared for in our home, mostly by my mother. I loved to give her food and watch her kitten playfulness. I named her Stripey as she was a tiger lookalike, but that was inevitably shortened to Pusspuss. There followed a guinea pig whose name was Guinea and a budgie whose name I don't recall. I was later told that I had a gift for healing animals, although at the time I wasn't aware of it.

As a young child, I was often sick. First, I contracted the usual colds and flu. I then went on to develop German measles, chicken pox, whooping cough, measles, and scarlet fever. With the exception of scarlet fever, I generously passed each on to John. I was six years old when my mother suffered what was probably a nervous breakdown resulting from stress and anxiety, not to mention the extra workload the accumulation of these illnesses caused her. A holiday was planned to help her recover. Off we set in my father's small car to the Cotswolds, with Nanna, my grandmother, in tow.

I should mention here that my father and my maternal grandmother had never seen eye to eye. They had an active dislike of each other which resulted in their avoidance of contact wherever possible. At this time, they were thrown together in their joint concern to help restore my mother's return to health and normality. During this tense time, there were the occasional spats. As if with swords drawn, they battled for the right to make the decisions needed to best restore harmony in the family.

We stayed at a rambling farmhouse and market garden which had been converted to accommodate guests for bed, breakfast, and evening meal. The meals were all prepared from fresh produce. Fruit, vegetables, and warm brown eggs. I was allowed to help collect them from the hen's nesting box (or wherever they chose to lay them throughout the garden). My outstanding memory of this holiday was seeing a paddock filled to overflowing with golden buttercups. I stood mouth agape in wonder. What sort of heaven was this? I wanted to remain here forever. I experienced such happiness, the kind that still resides in the recesses of my memory. I was also invited to watch the cattle being milked by hand. Along with my grandmother, I was given the opportunity to try this new skill, one I was unable to master. However, I enjoyed the closeness of their warm bodies, the sound of their chewing on the hay bales and watching the fresh milk filling the bucket. Golden happy days.

This break seemed to be what my mother needed and as we returned home, life appeared to gain some normality, although I began to sense the undercurrents of an unhappy household. I felt I could slice the tense atmosphere with a knife. It was also during my sixth year that I contracted scarlet fever and was confined to my small bedroom for six weeks. My brother John wasn't allowed near me for fear of him also coming down with it. As my body's immune system fought for control, my father sprayed my room each day and indeed the whole house in an attempt to contain the virus.

At last, I was well enough to get out of bed and peer at the outside world. I had a lovely view of our tiny lawn and the fields opposite. John and I were at last able to communicate as he played in the front garden. The smell of newly mown grass after a morning shower, the sight of red and orange dahlias lifting their faces to the summer sun and watching the wheat ripen in the distant meadow were all a joy to my starved senses. Then came the day I was finally well enough to venture down our narrow stairs and into the fresh air. How large everything looked from this new perspective and how good it was to feel the earth beneath my feet once more.

I was unaware of the food shortages that plagued us for many years following the end of that war. When my mother proudly brought home a pound of bananas (which she had queued for forty-five minutes to buy), I took one look at this alien, strangely shaped fruit and flatly refused to even take a small bite. How disappointed she must have been. However, my aversion receded over the years and I became very fond of this nutrient filled delight. I look back now at these childhood memories and smile, but these were difficult years not only for us but for a large part of the population. Many foods were rationed and much more were totally unavailable.

It was during one of those idyllic berry harvesting excursions that I experienced what I recall as the first lesson or insight from my life as an American Indian child. The luscious and enticing berries brought back a memory of a similar time when gathering the fruits of nature into a small woven container. The lesson told me, "eat the pure fruits of nature for they will nourish and sustain your body, mind, and spirit." It was instantaneous and fleeting but powerful enough to remain in my sub-conscious these past decades.

The second lesson or insight occurred one evening, again as a young child during the years of shortage following the Second World War. I was introduced to the craft of making rugs for the floor of our small home by cutting my mother's worn out stockings (which were thick 40 or 60 deniers) into strips and weaving this into a base of open weave fabric. I remember pausing one evening, with a flash, recalling being taught by my extended Indian family, the art of weaving, "teach this to your descendants to enhance their inherent creative abilities for future generations." An insight of things to come, as I subsequently used these skills when sewing and creating small garments for my own children as they grew, when money was in short supply.

My first days at school were a total shock. The regimentation and the discipline, so alien to my nature, bore down upon me. I was unable to answer my name at roll call, shrinking down in my seat, hoping no-one would notice me. On the third day, I decided I'd had enough. As mum kissed my cheek at the school gate, I ran as fast as my legs could carry me. I was followed by my teacher (who had witnessed my flight) and mum, who had promptly abandoned John in his pushchair. I was hauled back into the hated classroom and duly reprimanded. Mum continued to walk with me for several weeks until she felt I had settled in sufficiently. The task was then passed on to Martin, who lived next door. He was six and I adored him. The feeling, however, was not mutual. He accepted this burden reluctantly. After all, I was just a girl. Often he ran off and left me to drag my feet slowly up the hill to the torture called school. I advanced with difficulty. I made a friend or two but was painfully shy. My contribution to class activities was non-existent.

My paternal grandfather's garden was a continual source of delight. How I looked forward to time spent with him, learning how to nurture the vegetables he grew and when to harvest them. He taught me how to dig beneath the potato plant to see if the tubers were just right for eating. Although as an Indian child I had already learned these skills with yams and other wild treats that Mother Nature provided, this was a truly great refresher course. I revelled in these visits.

Grandfather, whom I loved dearly, spent his retirement cultivating a garden filled with an abundance of fragrant roses, lily of the valley and a lilac bush. Helping to harvest the many fruits and vegetables was a joy. Picking peas (and eating many straight from the pod), watching him turning the fertile earth, retrieving new potatoes and loading them into a bucket. Raspberries, plums, apples, and pears were plentiful from the small orchard at the top of the garden. The sweet perfume and the beauty of the lilac tree, along with the pure white lily-of-the-valley, still linger in my memory. They are forever stored in what my friend and mentor, Helen, later called my Treasure Chest of Memories. Accessible at any time of stress or anxiety to calm and bring solace to my troubled spirit.

My paternal grandparents were given one (or more) American soldiers to reside in their home after the US entered the war effort. I have no memory of their names, but one in particular, took a liking to me and noticed my lack of toys. I had only one doll, whose name was Pearl. She was my mother's when she was a child. Lovingly looked after, she was sizeable, with a china head and a wistful smile. This soldier set about making a wooden doll's cot, a wooden box of bricks and a push-along horse with a seat and a set of wheels which I named Dobbin. Such a kind and thoughtful thing to do.

Gypsies and superstitions

*Be aware to refrain from judgement of others, for we
are all one. We are all children of the Universe.*

My mother's side of the family was steeped in superstition, originating
from my grandmother. She didn't figure very much in my life until I
reached my teenage years. My mother stuck firmly to the superstitions
passed on to her. It was bad luck to walk under a ladder. Sensible, as the
workmen may have dropped something and caused injury. If you broke
a mirror, then seven years of bad luck will follow. This one struck fear

into my young mind and I became super-careful in my growing years and throughout my life not to cause such a catastrophe. If you spill salt, throw some over your left shoulder. To this day I'm not sure what dire fate awaited if I failed to do this. Crossing on the stairs was definitely banned. Yes, I guess you could miss your footing and fall. Always cross a Gypsy's palm with silver when they came to your door. If you failed to do this, very bad luck would follow.

It seems that choosing a day to cut your hair or nails will bode for you in the following way:

Cut them on a Monday, you cut them for health
Cut them on a Tuesday, you cut them for wealth
Cut them on a Wednesday, you cut them for news
Cut them on a Thursday, a new pair of shoes
Cut them on a Friday, you cut them for sorrow
Cut them on a Saturday, see your true love tomorrow
Cut them on a Sunday, the devil will be with you all the week

There are a few variations on that rhyme, but in all circumstances, cutting on a Sunday is cutting for evil. Ah, imagine what they would have thought about Sunday shopping.

Consequently, when a group of gypsies made camp a short way from our home, with their colourful Romany caravans, my mother was always super careful to have a shiny sixpence in her purse for that inevitability. My father forbade her from even opening the door when they came. However, in this instance, she defied him and the sixpence manifested some hand-made lace, a dozen or so wooden clothes pegs and a reading of her palm. I stood behind her skirts, totally in awe of this olive skinned wrinkled woman with her dark hair and long, brightly coloured, voluminous skirt. How she reminded me of my Native American Indian mother. I had no fear of her, only respect and a certain longing to be free of my current restrictive childhood and run free with the other barefooted children in the campsite.

As it happened, I needed to walk up that lane every day on my way to the primary school that I attended at the crest of the hill. My father's strict instructions were that I walk on the opposite side of the road as I passed the site and our neighbour's son (who was a year older than I) was asked to walk with me. However, he spurned my company and always ran on ahead much to my delight, for I preferred to walk alone. I meandered past the field where the gypsies were camped and smiled at the children who laughed and ran at will amongst the trees. I was somewhat of a curiosity to them with my blond curls and long limbs. They stared and pointed and laughed, and I in return laughed with happiness.

I never had a moment of fear of being abducted and not seen again, as my father had so sternly predicted. I felt akin to them as though I was part of their family, revelling in the warm scent of their horses who lazily grazed, or were exercised in the grassy fields. Their unique smell reminded me of the agile Indian ponies that I had loved. I was devastated when they were moved on, either by the local authorities or of their own free will. They were nomadic by nature, enjoying each stay, however brief, in the different areas of the English countryside.

It wasn't until many years later that I discovered humour and laughter. I seldom smiled and presented a serious countenance. I was so different from my friends and classmates who chatted and giggled through their teenage years. It was an effort on my part to join their mirth but I persisted with difficulty. Although I had two or three close friends, I was constantly and mercilessly teased and bullied at school. I was so different from the other students. I was quiet, shy, and sensitive. I preferred, for the most part, to be exploring nature and riding my much-loved bicycle along the quiet lanes. Or sitting beside a stream, watching the small fish and newly formed frogs, who were totally at home and tuned into their environment. It was at these times I felt connected with my inner self, Mother Nature, and the Universe. The warm fragrance of summer grass still has the power to evoke in me these memories of my childhood. Many times throughout my life I have felt more connected to my last life than with this one.

Intuition

*Ask and trust that answers will be given, but understanding
they are not always immediate. Be aware, alert and
focused, to receive the whispers of intuition.*

You may be thinking at this point, "I have no memories of my last life or
of any lessons or wisdom to help me, that I may pass on to my children
or to the people of this planet. How can I access any such information?"
In meditation you may be given insights or flashes of recall, be patient.
Many people have intuition which identifies certain places, events or

people as those not encountered in this present life. For example, have you visited a town or city for the first time, only to come across a house that is as familiar to you as your own? You instinctively know its layout, where the rooms are situated, their size and outlook. Or, having met someone, they seem vaguely familiar and you are tempted to ask, "have we met before?", knowing full well that you have not. Or you may have attended a meeting, a meal, or a function and thought "this conversation subject is so familiar to me."

My experiences and connections have been instantaneous, and at times took me by complete surprise. My most memorable regression and recognition was of my last life and occurred about eighteen years ago. I had travelled to a therapist in a suburb several miles from my home. The lady taught yoga and specialized in teaching stretching exercises which I was told would help my back pain. During the session, I became aware of a powerful spiritual presence which was confirmed as her primary Guide. I could see him as a celestial being clothed in a white robe with a white laser, which he directed to the areas of concern in my spine. Suddenly I had a flash of recognition and exclaimed, "I know you" to the therapist. Her name has long left my memory.

I saw her standing over me as my mother, in that last life which I loved so dearly. As I lay dying at age 12, I knew instantly that the insights and knowledge I had learned and experienced would travel with me into the spirit world and from there into my next life. I was overwhelmed with joy, as I knew she recognised me too. Although this meeting has been the only contact we have had, it has proved to be one of the most important and memorable thus far in this lifetime. These experiences or connections may not appear until you have mastered the art of a deep and profound meditative practice. You may be led to an experienced teacher for this to come to fruition.

Follow the path which best resonates with your intuition or it may be an instantaneous knowing as mine was. It may take weeks, months or even longer, but as you become more attuned, be assured that the memories and lessons will be given. Remember to ask for help from your guides with this – they are always willing and happy to assist. They will not interfere but will quickly respond to your requests. Try pre-programming your dreams. This can be most helpful and a lot of fun. Focus your mind on your desire to remember. Repeat the following several times before you go to bed, and again before you drift off to sleep, and then relax.

"I wish to be given access to the lessons I learned in my last life."

Or whatever sentence resonates with you. A symbol near your bed associated with what you want to access will help. Assemble a representation of positive lessons you may have gained in your last life. For example, love (heart), adventure (climbing a mountain), overcoming adversity (a mountain with you standing on the top). Make sure that you have your journal close by. If you wake in the night after a significant dream, write it down immediately as the memory of it may quickly fade. This technique can be used to help any problem you wish to solve. It may take practice, so try to be patient. Don't keep these lessons or insights to yourself, share them with the world, for you may be the carrier of valuable information to help one or many along their chosen life path.

Past life regression is one method of accessing past life memories. Choose a reputable practitioner, psychic, or clairvoyant to help you with this. Although it's not a hundred percent necessary to re-visit your past lives, many people find it helpful to dissipate any past life traumas you may have brought in with you. These may be limiting you or causing physical and/or emotional problems. Your higher self can be supportive with this, as it is possible to gain information either in a conscious or sleeping state. You may reap information or lessons, as I did, to help you move through present difficulties and obstructions to your well-being. Ask for help, either before you sleep or meditate. Make it specific. For example, *"I need to know what is causing my [insert]."* If you need further help to do this, I recommend that you contact a qualified practitioner who is able to assist with past life regression.

$\mathcal{T}$eenage

Nanna

Each day is a magical learning opportunity to move forward in wisdom and knowledge, through the eyes of a child.

As a small child, I felt my maternal grandmother paid little attention to me. She came to visit my mother on a weekly basis and presented a formidable figure with her black hair and eyes, and dark complexion. She reminded me of the gypsies and I studied her closely. I occasionally attempted to join the serious conversation, only to be met with a stern,

"Diana, your mother and I are talking. Don't interrupt." After such a rebuke, my shy and sensitive nature felt the words deeply and I retreated into my own thoughts.

However, as I grew and approached my teenage years, her interest in me seemed to blossom, as a bud opens after a spring shower. She became my new best friend and confidante. On occasional weekends and school holidays, I was invited to her home and was introduced to her world. She cooked and provided bed, breakfast and an evening meal for students at the nearby university. I watched with fascination as she cooked and presented their meals, carrying them into the dining room she had carefully prepared for their return each day. She patiently taught me to lay the table correctly, with cutlery for each course and a serviette neatly folded and rolled into silver serviette rings.

How I enjoyed those days, for she had many a tale to tell me. She also read tea leaves which was fascinating to me. My mind opened up and I clearly saw the intuition she shared from the pictures that the leaves portrayed. This was such a time of learning and expanding and I revelled in the knowledge she shared. The insights I gained from her interpretations were incredibly valuable and I have repeatedly been reminded of them throughout my life. Umbrellas frequently appeared, as did blossoms and buds. She explained that the umbrellas signified protection from the storms of life. The buds were a sign of opening to new possibilities and flowers the fruition of future knowledge and gifts.

She was a brilliant card player and could remember each one, as well as the order it had shown up in a game of whist or poker. Nanna occasionally took me to a whist drive and partnered me. This was to help me learn the game and to encourage and sharpen my memory. She had the gift of always winning the raffle, with the exception of one occasion, where I was asked to draw the winning ticket. I was astounded when I drew my own and proudly presented my winnings (a pair of beautiful turquoise drop earrings) to my mother upon returning home.

Nanna had great psychic ability and this experience was related to me by my mother. My grandfather was a salesman and travelled around the UK with his work. On one occasion he sourced a new home in East Anglia for nanna, mum, and Keith (who were young children at that time). Nanna had not seen the house, but on the day the family was due to move in, as she stepped inside the front door she exclaimed, "I can't live here!" I can only imagine his reaction. However, they discovered that two sisters, who had lived in the house previously, had both taken their own lives there. Nanna had felt the dark energies which remained in the house.

On one occasion, she took me to visit her mother's grave. I had met my great grandmother only once before she passed on from this life. My impression of her was of a distant persona, who said little. In retrospect I could see she had a dark aura, maybe resulting from stress and sadness in her life. I was to discover that my maternal ancestry in this lifetime is from the Indian sub-continent. My great, great grandmother was born in Bangalore, where she met, fell in love with, and married an Englishman.

My great, great grandfather's name was William. He joined the Regiment of Royal Lancers at the age of 19. His trade was a brush maker and his skills were in great demand. In fact, there were up to 7,000 such tradesmen in the UK in the 1800's. In 1876, he was transferred to Bombay with his regiment. Then in 1888 he was transferred to Bangalore, where he met his future Indian wife. They relocated to his homeland when his service in India was complete. How she must have suffered in that strange environment, from non-acceptance and lack of family support.

My mother had one brother, Keith, whom I adored. He was the epitome of the father I wished I had. When he visited our home, I was sure he could feel my admiring glances. My ears strained to catch his every word. His presence was one of gentle strength and seemingly unending knowledge and wisdom. He and his family lived some distance away, so

I rarely saw him. However, each visit was carefully and lovingly stored in my Treasure Chest of Memories.

My father worked different shifts each week. How we dreaded the weeks when he worked nights, for we would need to creep around like mice while he slept on the chair in the back room downstairs. If we were noisy he would burst into the hallway to abuse mum for not keeping us quiet. I would scurry away and hide until his tirade abated and he had retreated. He would close the door with two or three loud bangs, which shook our home to its foundations. On days such as this I wished with all my heart I could escape to an area of safety. My whole world seemed threatened and insecure. It literally rocked my sensitive nature to the core.

When I was nine my mother conceived my second brother, I was pleased only because in my childish mind, my father would no longer have the opportunity to display his rage. How wrong I was. Roy was born two weeks following my tenth birthday and mum spent the following week in hospital. I missed her badly. Her calming influence was my salvation throughout my childhood and early teenage years. This time, I felt no jealousy, but rather became his "little mother", taking him out in his pram and keeping him amused when I arrived home from school. Although he was a welcome addition to the family, I could feel the extra burden on my mother was a heavy one. There was also the added financial strain on my father's income.

My mother had acquired a bicycle for me. It was old, a little rusty, had a back pedal brake and one speed. It was my key to freedom and to exploring nature further afield. I was twelve years old, shy and introverted, but my joy at this small event was boundless and shone from my face like the sun, the stars, and the moon combined. However, I first needed to learn how to ride it. No mean feat, as even though I was tall for my age, my legs barely reached the pedals. Mum supported me by holding the seat and handlebars as I bravely pedalled with all my strength. Eventually, she was able to release her firm grip without my being aware and off I went, rejoicing in this new achievement. What a strange sight we must have portrayed. However, the joy of achievement glowed from me, eradicating any embarrassment I may have felt.

One of my favourite places to go was the woodland a few miles away from our home. I spent many hours sitting quietly beside the stream that flowed through the trees. I was in awe of the beauty and the peace which enveloped me. Songbirds and small animals would approach without fear. Many years later I was told I had been a healer of both people and animals since childhood and in fact, my healing gift was permanently switched on.

My early teenage years heralded a desire to begin nurturing and growing plants. I began with bean seeds in a narrow-necked glass jar. I watched fascinated, as the first sign of small white roots appeared, closely followed by young green shoots. This was followed by hyacinth bulbs grown in the same fashion. Soon I graduated to growing pumpkin and squash in our small back garden. Such delight followed as first they bore flowers and then the plump juicy crop, which we eagerly consumed.

Moving into my passion

Some of My Botanical Paintings

Follow your passion and your divine life purpose. Joy,
happiness, peace, and contentment will follow.

Looking back over my growing years, I now realise that although I was unable to see them, I was consciously communing with Nature Spirits. What a privilege these experiences had been. An initiation into my spiritual development in this lifetime, as well as the gateway which opened to receiving and remembering the lessons from my last life.

These were then unconsciously stored in my inner being to be released over the coming years, culminating in the knowledge that now is the time to share them with all mankind.

It was during this time I came to the realisation of my future vocation. My passion for nature exploded, as well as my need for a place to grow and propagate my growing collection of cacti, succulents, and annual seedlings. The desire for a small glasshouse began to surface and take shape, but how to obtain one? Having thought it through in my young teenage mind, I determined to find a Saturday job. With the help of my mother, I scanned the advertisements and eventually came across "Saturday help wanted for cactus nursery." How perfect. I determined this job was to be mine. Mum and I caught two buses to the interview. I was enraptured by the diversity and volume of the plants that were neatly displayed on benches throughout three large glass houses. I felt as though I was in heaven.

Success. I was hired after displaying my considerable knowledge of plant care. Off I pedalled each Saturday on my trusty bicycle. A twenty-minute ride, rain or shine, to spend four blissful hours weeding, watering and giving loving attention to all in my care. These precious hours reinforced the feeling that I was in heaven. Then, suddenly I had sufficient funds for a small greenhouse which needed to be erected on-site in our tiny overgrown garden at the rear of our house. Now I had to ask my father to help. Needless to say, mum had paved the way and it was done over one weekend, not without a little angst from my father. I stood gamely to one side and gritted my teeth as he vented his feelings on the wooden structure.

Joy. I moved my small collection in and began the happy task of seed sowing, taking cuttings and maintaining my growing collection. I was sternly warned not to let this time spent with my plants interfere with my studies. I endeavoured to maintain a balance, yet always prioritised my school work. This was easy to do. I knew I had a peaceful place to escape to when the atmosphere in our house was too tense to bear.

In my remaining years at school, I worked hard to gain the scholastic qualifications to enable me to be accepted into a horticultural college, gain my diploma and follow my calling.

I was not gifted with a photographic memory as was my brother John. How I looked up to him and admired him as he studied Latin, maths, and chemistry, all of which seemed so far out of my reach. However, I studied hard and succeeded in all my subjects, with maths being the exception. My teacher wisely advised me to stop spending the majority of my time on something I had no hope of ever grasping. I looked back with gratitude. The anxiety I suffered over not understanding the mysteries of algebra and geometry was taken from me. I left school and along with two friends, went for a well-earned holiday to Devon on the south coast of England. The weather was superb, warm and sunny. I experienced the happiness of my achievement and the anticipation of the years ahead, working in the environment I loved.

However, my happiness was soon to be shattered when a letter from my mother arrived, telling me my beloved grandfather had passed on. I was devastated and inconsolable. How I would miss him. Ultimately I realised he was following my progress throughout the years as one of my ancestral guides. This knowledge was not apparent (or given to me) for some time, but has served to comfort and uplift me in the difficult years which followed.

I had secured a full-time position at a local nursery. This covered the twelve-month period of practical experience I needed before heading off to college. It was owned and managed by a family who befriended me. The hours were long and the work, although initially menial, was demanding. Their specialities were glasshouse mop-head chrysanthemums, being the crop of the autumn and winter months, peaking at Christmas time. They were in great demand as cut flowers as they lasted a full month. I loved watching them develop from a small bud to their full glory, and took great joy in my nurturing role. The summer crop was tomatoes. My hands were permanently green, from the leaves and stems and from harvesting the lush red fruit. How the time flew. I had saved from my meagre wage. It was enough to help pay for my college fees. I also gave half to my mother for food and board as I knew money was scarce. My youngest brother Roy was now seven years old.

It was during this time I began to date my first boyfriend, who was a lay preacher at the Methodist church where I taught Sunday school. He asked if I would like to play tennis one evening. Having played at school, I had some skill and knowledge of the game, so I accepted. So began a short relationship and a steep learning curve into what I did not want in a future partner. Thankfully we lost touch as I moved into my college year, but not before tears and heartache had haunted my waking moments.

College and beyond

Let your dreams lead you to find your place
of fulfilment and peace.

The time finally came for me to depart for my college year at age seventeen. How I had looked forward to this time. The knowledge I would acquire and the joy of working with Mother Earth. I was never to return to live at the small country home of my childhood years. The students all had a small room big enough to accommodate a bed, with a side table and a desk for study. The college was located in what was originally a sizable country estate. It had been divided into orchards, glasshouses, potting sheds, lecture rooms and acres of vegetables.

It was here that I experienced my first encounter with a spirit or ghost, as I walked along the corridors of our quarters to the shower room. I felt an energy brush past my shoulder, firm enough to turn my upper body a little. I turned to look but saw no-one. This experience, rather than frighten me, fascinated me and opened me to other more intense encounters. In an instant, I had a flash of understanding of other planes of existence and of the spirit world and what lay between.

My year at college literally flew by and I eagerly absorbed every piece of information that was presented at lectures, with the exception of crop protection. This involved, for the most part, spraying the crops with toxic chemicals. It never sat well with me. Why add this toxicity to nature's bounty and her gift of nutritious energy? I was soon to learn of companion planting and organic pest control.

As my year at college drew to an end, we were all given a list of available positions. One, in particular, drew my attention. It was on the outskirts of London but looked a peaceful environment. It beckoned me. Little did I guess how dramatically this decision would change my life. I applied and was accepted on the strength of the diploma I had gained. I began to search for a share situation within my meagre price range. A room became available in a small townhouse within a short distance from my future workplace. Perfect. Happiness welled in my heart. I had no wish to return to my childhood home. Although I knew I would miss my mother.

I shared this small apartment with a forty-something-year-old physiotherapist, who had never married. I had my own room, but she cooked us both an evening meal. Again, my trusty bike faithfully carried me to and from work. With the exception of days and sometimes weeks when the inclement English climate caused me to take a bus and walk the remainder of the way. My work involved helping to tend the garden, interspersed with time in the office. It was discovered I had an artistic gift and I worked on sketches for the owner's books.

The extensive grounds and gardens were based solely on organic culture, using no pesticides, herbicides or chemical fertilisers. I realised it was many years ahead of its time, as few ventures of that era were run in this way. It comprised of several acres of vegetables, fruit and flower beds. Companion planting protected crops vulnerable to pests and diseases. Compost from green household vegetable matter and clean vegetative garden trimmings ensured vigorous healthy growth. Initially, I felt honoured to be part of this important venture. But as I was to discover, this wasn't to be an easy time for me. It was challenging, as the owner was overbearing and somewhat of a bully towards his staff.

It was during this time that I met and fell in love with my future husband, Ron. I was 19, he was 33 and seemed kind and thoughtful. A father figure? Maybe. He courted me and we spent every weekend together. He took me to clubs in the city. As a country girl at heart, I found them noisy and overwhelming. However, we also enjoyed meals and long talks, as well as joining a ballroom dancing class. Here I was in my element. Although not with bare feet on the earth, I once again felt the connection with Mother Earth and my spirits rose.

My employer's behaviour became increasingly difficult for me to cope with and I knew it was time to move on and find a better job. The perfect solution came when I was offered a position in a research institute some distance from the city, but not impossible for Ron to make the trip to visit. The elderly lady with whom I shared, was amenable and allowed Ron to share an evening meal in my small sitting room. Shortly afterwards we became engaged and my parents suggested a party to celebrate not only this event but the occasion of my twenty-first birthday. I was overcome with happiness and once again looked forward to a future which I could only see as being endlessly blissful. Little did I know this would be far removed from the truth.

We married on the fourth of July. A sunny summer's day, that held hope and promise, confetti and roses. I was radiantly happy as we bade farewell to family and guests and headed off on our honeymoon. However, as I quickly discovered, I was totally naïve to the concept of married life and had difficulty tuning into the needs, ideas, and demands of my new husband. I had no idea how to cook anything. When I lived at home, my mother had scarce time to teach me in the tiny kitchen and I showed little interest. My mind was focussed in another direction. I persevered.

We lived in a small apartment on the first floor of an old suburban house in the northern suburbs of London. It was dark, damp and cold, but it was our home. I absolutely loved my new work and a colleague who lived nearby offered to drive me there and back, in exchange for petrol money. It was a perfect arrangement which saved me a train journey, a bus ride, and a half mile walk, twice a day. I had my own office and was in charge of various projects, both in the extensive glasshouses and open vegetable plots. My workmates and I soon became friends, enjoying tea breaks and lunch hours, chatting and exchanging viewpoints on every imaginable subject.

The days flew by. I was immersed in my work and the joy of learning new skills at home. I became a passable cook, putting together meals that looked appetising and seemed to please Ron. I also began to sew and embroider table runners, cushion covers, and bedspreads, in preparation for the time we would buy our own home. However, this was not to be. I discovered Ron had little or no savings from his well-paid job. This didn't disturb me at the time, but later when I found the reason, I began to be concerned.

The accident

Is this a cosmic accident? No. There are no mistakes, only opportunities to learn.

That winter was one that had a plentiful supply of ice and snow. Our journey to work took us along country lanes where snow ploughs had no access. Carol had little experience with such conditions. On this fateful morning, her little car skidded on a corner and mounted a bank, almost overturning. Having no seat belt I was thrown around the car. I heard myself scream as we landed with a bang back on the road. I felt my spine crack and the pain that followed was excruciating. Fortunately, Carol wasn't injured as she had been able to brace herself on the steering wheel.

I was in shock, unable to move or speak, staring at the road, not even comprehending what had just occurred. After what seemed an eternity, Carol turned to me to ask if I was ok, but seeing I was not, realised she needed to seek help. I shivered with cold and shock until she eventually returned. The ambulance took us to the nearest hospital where we were both thoroughly checked and I was wheeled off to the X-Ray department. I sustained fractured vertebrae, a twisted pelvis, whiplash, and a double thoracic scoliosis, although I wasn't told the extent of my injuries at that time.

The doctor came to stick pins in my legs each day, to ascertain whether there was a spinal cord injury. This proved not to be so but was the beginning of two months lying on my back while the fractures healed. Nothing could be done at that time to straighten my pelvis or adjust the scoliosis which continued to give me pain for many years. At no time did I question why this has happened to me, I just knew I needed to get well. I had work to do in this life. I later realised, much to my surprise, I had never spoken to anyone about that.

Ron arrived distressed. My mother travelled to see me and stood beside my bed with tears streaming down her face. I, however, showed no sign of emotion for three days. On the fourth day, I began to sob. Not a cry, but a full on release. The matron was summoned and asked if someone had upset me, I was able only to shake my head. Delayed shock had set in, which lasted most of the day.

My nurses were absolutely wonderful and did their best to make me smile. There was one particular nurse whom we all loved. How could we not? She was a petite South African with a smile as wide as the sky, revealing white even teeth. We called her Sunny. Every day she sashayed into our ward and brought sunshine into our days. Such was her effect on me that I still see her face radiating love and compassion. These moments helped me work through the pain and restriction of my life at that time. Bed baths were a trial, I hated anyone seeing my bare body, the nurses just laughed and told me "We have seen so many. To us, it's just a body." I gradually became more adjusted to this routine. Being fed and sipping my liquids through a straw. However, bedpans were altogether a nightmare. I became chronically constipated as any effort caused more pain. As the days passed, different patients came and went (I shared the ward with three others) and we exchanged thoughts daily about the state of our health and our pain levels. This proved a comfort, in varying degrees, for each of us.

Winter turned to spring and as the light filled ward took on a new vibration of promise, my spirits lifted. I would soon be well enough to return to our home. A final X-Ray confirmed this and my belongings were neatly stowed in my bag. This eagerly anticipated day had arrived. The nurses came to bid me farewell and I shed a tear as I thanked them for their care. However, I was unable to walk. My muscles had wasted and I had lost a tremendous amount of weight. I was supported on both sides as I took my first steps towards regaining my strength and mobility.

Our apartment had the feel of neglect and damp reigned supreme. Even with the meagre warmth of the small electric fire, I suffered from the cold. My mother came to stay for a week or two. This cheered me and alleviated my lonely days. She cooked and cleaned and washed, it was a huge comfort for me. Although I spent much of my time resting, I gradually began to walk a little further each day. How I longed to be able to sit in the garden beneath the sycamore tree and breathe in the spring air. It was then I rediscovered my love of reading. I read about nature and I read fiction. The story that impressed me most was set in Devon, on the south coast. Little did I know that we would soon be living in that area.

As spring turned to summer, I was able to return to work. I had been fortunate to have been paid for some of my extended recovery time. However, I had only returned for a few weeks when the news was announced that my workplace was to be relocated to the east coast. At this point, we decided to move out of London. Ron had a desire to start his own business. We took a holiday to Devon, ostensibly to research business opportunities. I fell in love with the rolling green hills and the fresh country air was nectar to my soul. We had taken a tent and camped out each night to save money. Towards the end of our trip, we pitched camp at a small site overlooking the ocean. A perfect location. It was here I conceived my first child.

Having found it to be a suitable work area, the decision was made. As we made preparation for what was to be a momentous relocation, I began to feel unwell. Nausea overtook my days. A visit to the doctor confirmed my pregnancy. Shock. I actively disliked children, as a result of being mercilessly teased by a group of youngsters when in my early teens. However, Ron seemed pleased and accepted the news calmly. We began the search for rented accommodation. We scoured notice boards and newspaper advertisements. Having visited three, we decided on a small stone cottage with an ocean view, nestled in a sloping valley on a farm estate. It was quiet and remote, yet close enough to commute to Plymouth.

The ground floor consisted of a large kitchen with an Aga stove and an ample living room. Up a narrow flight of stairs were three small bedrooms and a bathroom. These were accessed by a narrow corridor under the sloping roof. I was in awe of the view and of the walled garden and rockery which surrounded the building. I looked forward to being able to grow flowers and vegetables once my baby was born and the rampant weeds had been cleared. The day finally arrived and we departed in our small car followed by two friends carrying the remainder of our belongings on the journey to our new home.

As autumn morphed into winter, the stream of friends and family who visited dwindled and stopped. I became increasingly lonely. I had not as yet learnt to drive and our nearest neighbour was a good half mile walk along a rough track. The locals looked upon us as visitors from "the Big Smoke" and we found their broad Devonshire accent challenging to understand. My one outing of the week was to shop for food in the village. I craved company. Ron began to go out each night, with Sunday being the only exception. I spent my time sitting by the Aga to keep warm, knitting tiny vests and layettes with ribbons that tied at the front. I was given an old style treadle sewing machine and took to making maternity clothes. As I grew in size my spinal pain returned. I rested each afternoon so that I could ease it enough to cook our evening meal.

During this time, I became an avid cook, experimenting with recipes from the book I had been given as a wedding gift. Soon I became quite accomplished, even trying my new found skills with baking bread. The local baker who delivered to our door was occasionally unreliable. To top it off, he left the gate open to our garden. The cattle were delighted and trooped in to sample fresh grass and generally trample throughout our garden. We had to call one of the farm hands, who herded them out with a few swear words of encouragement.

Eventually, I became friends with the farmer's wife a mile or so from our home. I walked, or rather waddled, over for afternoon tea and a much-needed chat. She had a young baby and was most helpful in teaching me how to fold a cloth nappy and pin it without piercing the baby's skin. Mostly I practiced on a banana. This brought back memories of my mother's foray and my first reaction to this fruit. It brought a smile to my lips, and comfort to my soul. Then it snowed and I was once more isolated. Phone calls were my only contact with the outside world. Standing by our kitchen window, the loneliness overtook me once more. My only consolation was the beauty of the pristine white landscape across the fields stretching to the ocean. I longed to leave the house but was fearful of falling and further injuring my back and my unborn child.

Spring eventually arrived and despite my increasing size, my spirits lifted. Visitors returned in a steady stream and I cooked, cleaned and waited. Much to my delight, the hedgerows burst into bloom with primroses, violets and a multitude of wild flowers. I watched as newly born calves and foals circled their mothers. I rejoiced in the knowledge that my time would soon come. I was offered a lift to the tiny church hall once a week. Here, myself and several other mums-to-be were taught how to breathe during labour and what to expect with the birth. I was awestruck and overwhelmed.

Motherhood

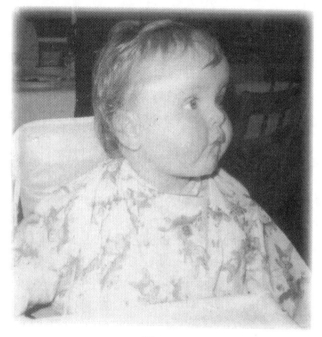

Karen

Motherhood is a gift from the Universe and to be cherished
as sunshine after rain or calm after a storm.

Early in April, there was more snow and it was then I felt the first pains
at 4am on what threatened to be a cold, windy day. There had been
no movement for three or four weeks from my baby, but the doctor
assured me the heartbeat was strong. We rushed to the hospital, a forty-
five-minute drive along country lanes. Fear and anticipation filled me.

However, after a while, the pain eased and then stopped altogether. With disappointment in my heart, I was sent home. Another week passed and we were off again, this time for real. I was installed in a tiny windowless room with only a bed and a chair. Ron sat by my side as my labour progressed, only leaving to eat. First breakfast, then lunch, and finally an evening meal.

It was during that last meal my time had come to deliver my baby. I was wheeled into the delivery room by silent and unresponsive nursing staff. Finally, she arrived. A beautiful girl. I was ecstatic. As she was handed into my arms, her piercing blue eyes met mine and my love for my daughter overflowed. I heard myself say "I love you", she smiled a gentle, all-encompassing smile. My active dislike of children was instantly transformed into a deep irrevocable love for this tiny child. Indeed, my perspective was forever altered towards all children.

Then the heartaches and joys of motherhood began. At two days old the doctor discovered she had misshapen feet that turned inward. No wonder she was unable to move during those last few weeks. They had been caught, one over the other in the restricted area of my womb. She was immediately fitted with plaster casts from her feet to her knees. The nurses nicknamed her Bootsie, which didn't altogether ease my distress. At that time, the doctors hadn't found that her hips were also badly affected. I was the only new mum in the ward who chose to breastfeed my baby. I endeavoured to do so quietly each night in order not to disturb the other mums whose babies were taken off to the nursery at bedtime.

Although she had no difficulty in gaining back her birth weight, Karen was a slow feeder taking up to an hour each feed. Then there were an additional thirty minutes to bring up her wind. I was exhausted during those first months, dragging my tired aching body through each day in a haze of exhaustion. My spinal pain had returned with a vengeance, all I wanted to do was rest. As every new mother knows, our lives change dramatically and we all but drown in endless piles of washing, feeding, and concern for our newborn's well-being. Rather than feeling overwhelmed, I overcame the exhaustion and revelled in the challenge. This tiny new child would be nurtured and loved with all my heart and soul. Washing was a twice daily event and standing over our little twin tub machine was traumatic. I began to understand and appreciate how mum had coped with only a tub and a handwringer for all the washing my brothers and I had produced. Not to mention my father's shirts and collars, which had to be starched and ironed to perfection.

It was necessary for me to take Karen to the hospital weekly for the doctors to assess her progress in straightening her little feet. Whilst there, my gratitude overflowed as I saw many other babies with problems that were a lot worse. Initially, I felt no-one was having such a difficult time as I in trying to cope with my child's disability. After two months the plasters were taken off and tapes were added which made it easier at bath time. At eighteen months old, they were discarded altogether. It was then that the hip displacement came to light. A brace was made to be fitted and worn continually. She was able to sit comfortably with her legs splayed apart but sleeping was a challenge for her.

Once again my heart broke to see my precious child in this situation. However, she remained happy to play with the toys we surrounded her with and seemed content with hours of solitary amusement as I chatted to her whilst cooking, washing, and cleaning. I found it increasingly difficult to lift and carry her as she eagerly accepted the food I provided, with the exception of vegetables which she duly spat out, much to my concern. This time without exercise led to her gaining weight and she became a chubby pre-toddler. In fact, she wasn't able to walk until she was more than three years old. I considered we were very blessed. The doctors told me that if she had been born fifty years earlier, she would have been a cripple all her life.

I became pregnant with my second child when Karen was two years and three months old. Additional stress on my spine increased as my pregnancy advanced. The weight of Karen on my hip was hard to bear.

Nevertheless, I was happy and looked forward to the birth of this new baby. I begged my doctor to give his permission for me to have my baby at home as I dreaded the rigours of the hospital labour room and the new mother's ward. Thankfully, permission was given.

I soon realised I needed to learn to drive. This was no mean feat, as I still carried fear and dread of a further accident. The lanes were narrow and vision was poor due to the tall hedgerows and undulating countryside. The roads seemed to lazily bend and turn at will. However, hiding my fear, I embarked on a course of lessons. With Karen safely installed in her carrycot on the back seat, I ventured forth. My instructor was patient and understanding, and I soon gained confidence.

The day of my test dawned hot and sunny. I virtually shook with nerves. The driving test inspector was a burly, six foot two, ex-CID policeman. He literally folded himself into our mini. With his head touching the roof, we set off. I was certain he could see my hands shaking. With difficulty, I managed to remember the tips and tricks my instructor had so carefully instilled in me. As we drove into the parking area, I waited with bated breath while he completed his notes. I had passed. Such was my relief, I leaned forward, put my forehead on the steering wheel and burst into tears. In spite of his (and my) embarrassment, he kindly patted my arm and handed me the paperwork.

Now I could independently take Karen to the hospital and venture out into the local village for our weekly shopping. Such a sense of relief flooded over me. I felt this achievement was really something to be proud of. However, my confidence was short-lived. I found negotiating the winding lanes on my own was stressful. As with the many challenges, both past and future, I persevered and overcame. However, it was some time before I negotiated the roads, and indeed this life, with a degree of self-confidence.

Mum arrived two weeks before my due date. I was so thankful for her help, as I was huge. I was all out at the front and found bending impossible. Intuition told me this baby was ready to be born, even though it was nearly two weeks before my due date. A little unwillingly, mum accompanied me to the chemist in the small village. I purchased a bottle of castor oil, for I had read it would lubricate and speed labour. Success. It worked. My waters broke at 4am the following morning and the midwife was summoned. Mum was an emotional mess, not knowing whether to pace the floor, make tea, or remain in the background. How I loved her for persevering. The midwife chatted amiably. I was grateful for this diversion from the painful spasms.

Eventually, she felt it was time to migrate to our bedroom, but first a bath. She instructed mum to help me as I heaved my swollen body into the water, she was not a little embarrassed, but I was past embarrassment. I just needed to move through this as quickly as possible. Then at lunchtime, he was here, my beautiful wrinkled baby boy. Not at all like Karen, he was covered in a black coating and I wasn't allowed to hold him immediately. My disappointment and distress were evident, in spite of the doctor's assurance that he was ok and this would soon disappear. Exhaustion set in and I craved sleep. It was not to be, as Karen was returned from my friend's care and was full of questions. She was somewhat taken aback at the appearance of this tiny being.

Looking back, this was the turning point in my marriage. Ron seemed to lose interest and patience, not only with me but with life in general. He seemed restless and had begun to go out each night, refusing to tell me where and with whom. I felt neglected. I dragged myself through days of washing, cleaning, cooking and looking after my children. After a while, I almost became adjusted to this new aspect of our marriage. I compensated by enjoying the countryside and the abundant flora which adorned hedgerows and paddocks. I also continued to knit and sew each evening. Small dresses for Karen and jumpers for Kyle. But, best of all, I rediscovered dance. We had an old record player and when my babies were taking their afternoon sleep, I would play my favourite music and dance to my heart's content. I was re-establishing my connection with the rhythm of Mother Earth. I felt a surge of joy as images and sounds from my last life coursed through my veins and my very soul. Thus, I temporarily created my own happiness. This and my love for my babies sustained me.

I have always loved to dance, to move to the rhythm of the music, or just for pure joy and letting go of pent up energy. As a child, it was tap-dancing. I still have the memory of my much-loved tap shoes, dancing for nanna and blossoming under her admiring gaze. As a young adult, it was ballroom and jive. One day, quite suddenly, I realised with delight why it made me feel so good. A vision of my last life opened and I saw myself dancing barefoot, feeling the rhythm of Mother Earth flowing through me. Her energy literally taking me into a higher sense of awareness and connection to the unconditional love of the Universe. This realisation was to be the first in a series of intuitive messages or lessons I had brought with me into this life.

Decisions

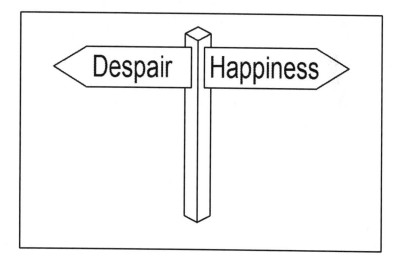

We are given free choice in our lives. Always listen
for guidance in order to make wise decisions.

Communication became sparse between Ron and I and my efforts to re-establish our harmonious relationship were in vain. I felt abandoned. Our meal times were relegated to a strict timetable of 1pm for lunch and 6pm for the evening meal. No later. I cried out for help and suggested we go to a marriage counsellor. He agreed, but the visits achieved little. I was often in tears as I saw our marriage begin to crumble before my very eyes. My access to the phone and car were limited. Although occasionally I rang mum, I felt unable to tell her what was happening in my life. However, I knew she must have guessed.

Ron's attitude toward me began to change. I was treated more as a combined possession and housekeeper. Following our evening meal, he would leave, not returning until well after midnight. I was not privy to any information of his whereabouts and my enquiries were met with "It's none of your business." Soon this escalated into disconnection of the phone while he was out, preventing me from contacting friends and also my mother. I sent thanks every night that the children were not sick as I would have been unable to summon help, such was the remoteness of our home. This was followed by disabling of the car if I hadn't abided by the rules. For a while, I rebelled but this only brought more restrictions. Following my protests, I was ignored for days, as if I was not even there.

At this point, I began a secret life. I needed company, compassion, and understanding. I turned to friends for help. I was fearful of being discovered but persisted as a drowning man clinging to a lifeline. On my weekly trip to shop for food, I visited my friend Estelle, whose marriage was also in trouble. We took comfort in one another's woes. A short while later she introduced me to her colleague, a real estate businessman. We became friends and I was offered part time work promoting his business. In the days before computers and the internet appeared this involved phone calls and securing appointments from his office. Karen was now six and was at school and Kyle was accepted into kindergarten three mornings a week. This part time work made my life more bearable. I was not one to simply give up.

Eventually, Ron told me I could work there no longer. He had seen the lift in my mood and demeanour. I refused and the physical abuse began. I was covered in bruises and began to fear for my life, following threats that were screamed at me. In retrospect, this was my lowest point. I had to get away. But how, and where? There were no shelters at that time for women such as myself and I knew my father would not accept us into his home. So it was, that I began to look for a haven. A place I could go and resume a peaceful and productive life with my children.

Friends have often asked, "How did you survive this heartache, the hard work, and the disappointment?" I had a mission in this life, not only to survive but to thrive. To share the lessons and insights I had been given and were still arriving in my conscious and dreaming state. Kyle often asked, "Mummy, why do you always cry now?" How could I explain to this sensitive, caring child? I have since come to understand the hardest and most difficult times in your life have the ability to build your resilience and sense of purpose.

I knew I had to leave, the threats became dark and ominous, the physical abuse escalated and my spirit was all but broken. But where to go? My doctor was unable to help, even when I turned up with bruises and injuries. Then, out of the blue, an opportunity was presented through a friend. She had previously introduced me to a businessman whom I had helped with promotional literature from time to time. I was aware of his feelings towards me and the ambitious nature of his projects. His colleagues in Australia had prompted him to extend his empire to New South Wales. He proposed that I follow when he had become established, in essence, to work and build a new life for myself and my children. In retrospect, Ron and I had little in common. We were ill-matched and initially I was too young and lacking in experience to see it. Ron was the father figure I had lacked and longed for in my childhood. He was fourteen years my senior and I was attracted to his seemingly mild, compassionate nature.

Leaving him was a huge decision, maybe one of the most challenging and life changing I could ever have contemplated. I told no-one, while I researched and gathered information about my proposed new country. The diversity of opportunities which abounded there were infinitely attractive, as was the temperate climate in New South Wales. However, I knew I must consider my children. Karen was seven and Kyle four. They were due to begin school the following year. How would this move affect their wellbeing and future development? I considered the alternative. Living in fear of my life would surely affect them. It all but broke my heart.

The decision was made and I began the necessary arrangements. Mum and I spent a few days in Nanna's caravan on the South Coast and it was there that I told her. Her shock was evident. She knew I had been unhappy but I had hidden the truth, not feeling able to share the extent of my distress and Ron's physical and emotional cruelty. I felt extreme sadness in telling of this revelation so close to our departure. I endeavoured to reassure her we would be okay.

I had nurtured my belief that I had a divine purpose in this life and had already begun to see visions of many people reaching out to me for help. However, it was to be many years before I was able to fulfil this calling. At last, after a tearful farewell, we were on our way. A sense of relief flooded my being. My children felt my sense of excitement but the long flight exhausted us all. We slept fitfully until touching down in Darwin at 2am. The plane was sprayed for insects over the heads of the passengers. This was due to customs regulations at that time. We disembarked while our aircraft was refuelled. The warm night air filled my lungs. As I looked up at the array of stars, it took my breath away. I was home.

A new life

Your star will shine brightly in the darkness,
providing guidance in times of need.

Four hours after leaving Darwin, we arrived in Sydney to torrential rain. We were met and driven to the house David had leased. He suggested we live together until I could find an apartment of my own. I was too exhausted to argue. So began a short affair which ended as soon as it had begun. The business venture had initially taken off well but after three months it failed suddenly and irrevocably.

I had grown to love this area, with its beautiful beaches and laidback lifestyle. Karen had been enrolled and had commenced school, and Kyle accepted into kindergarten. I had made friends with Vera and Daniel, as well as one or two business associates. I now searched for accommodation which was inexpensive and close to a bus route and the school. The search manifested a small unfurnished two-bedroom apartment. I desperately needed a job that would enable me to take and meet my children from school and kindergarten. I had no money and we had no furniture. I managed to borrow enough for four weeks' rent, food, and kindergarten fees and set about job hunting.

At the end of that week, I had sixty cents and had secured a job at a local small business. I helped with bookkeeping and daily takings. Twenty hours a week didn't bring in enough money to keep us. Then, out of the blue, a position became available for two nights' reception duties at a club nearby. My panic subsided, but now I needed a babysitter for those two evenings. Again, I was blessed with an answer to my prayers. I was being supported by the Universe and felt re-assured. My neighbour had two children of similar ages, and we became lifelong friends. We shared our struggles, she with her husband and I with my frugal income, lack of security and meagre furniture.

We had been given beds for each of us, which was a huge blessing. We were also given a small table and three chairs for the living area along with some bedding. I bought towels at a closing down sale for a few cents and summer clothing at the local Red Cross shop. Somehow we would survive. I was happy to be free from the fear which had hounded me for so long. I was determined to build a good life for myself and my children. How I loved our new home. Though small, it somehow provided a haven at the end of the day. We were on the first floor with a small balcony and trees outside the window, a perfect outlook for my weary spirit.

Gratitude flowed through me – we had been protected and supported by the Universe. I stored this knowledge in my heart and it sustained me through this time of financial lack and hardship. I gained inspiration and strength from a book called *Jonathan Livingstone Seagull* which I borrowed from a friend. I read it avidly on the bus to and from work. I loved the clear wide sky, the golden beaches, and the warmth of the sun on my face. This land seemed to embrace me with its sometimes stark beauty, radiant vibration, and smiling inhabitants. Most nights after work, I was so exhausted, that I would lie on the living room floor and fall asleep before I had enough energy to prepare our evening meal. This regularly consisted of soup (often tomato) followed by a boiled egg each and fingers of toast which we called "Soldiers". Not surprisingly to this day, Karen has an aversion to tomato soup.

I later realised I had suffered from adrenal fatigue, such as experienced by many women in their 30's, 40's and 50's who not only care for their families and often ageing parents but also work at thankless jobs to pay the never ending bills. Nevertheless, I loved our little home, it's energy wrapped itself around us like a protective shield. I made curtains for the balcony windows, which enveloped us in cosiness during dark evening hours. Initially, I found it somewhat difficult to adjust to the different daylight hours. Summer days began with a 5am dawn and ended with an 8.30pm sunset. Winter was 7am to 5pm.

I soon learned to adapt and become in tune. My evening shifts at the club were my social life. I did receive invitations and advances from various male members and staff. However, when I became aware of their marital status, I had no desire to disrupt or endanger their marriages. We walked to the park or the beach on the weekends and our occasional treat was a refreshing fruity ice block. I met other single mothers and my sense of equilibrium returned, there were many in similar circumstances as myself. Abuse and cruelty were never spoken of, but their eyes betrayed their inner sadness.

Then I became sick. Panic. I can't be sick. But I was. Very sick. In fact, I was so ill that I couldn't get out of bed. Karen helped Kyle get ready in the morning and they both walked to and from school accompanied by the children from next door. Evening meals consisted of a sandwich. Two weeks later, I began to improve and pushed myself to return to work. The bills had mounted and I was unable to pay the rent. I promised to catch up as soon as I could. I was fastidious about paying on time and this added burden weighed heavily on me. I still refused to ask my father for his help. My pride and determination to survive surpassed every instinct. Again, we survived. Gradually I managed to repay my debts by cutting out any expense I deemed unnecessary.

Although not fully recovered, and getting to the surgery would be a challenge, I made an appointment with the doctor. A large red swelling had appeared close to my left eye. The elderly physician took one look at me and prescribed a tonic and a cream for the swelling. As he told me the cost, I burst into tears. I couldn't pay the $10 (approximately $150 by today's value). Seeing my distress, he told me to pay him when I could. Such an act of kindness renewed my tears, this time, tears of gratitude. I vowed to repay the loan, which I did, although it took four months to do so.

Suddenly it was Christmas and parties were in full swing. I was invited to several, but I was unable to afford a child-minder. My two evenings work as a receptionist substituted for my social life. However, I did accept one invitation and spent two hours after my shift at a beautiful waterfront party. That two hours lifted my spirits. I joined in the conversation and had the most wonderful time. Thus far, I had yet to realise that I was attracting the interest of one or two hopeful suitors. My life had been filled with work and caring for my children. I had failed to recognise the fact that I was an attractive young woman. A Christmas tree appeared in our living room with a five-dollar note hidden in its branches.

I felt incredibly blessed and rich but wasn't ready to begin a relationship. Past experiences were too fresh in my mind. We were invited to spend Christmas day with my friend, her husband, and their two adorable poodles. Such a happy day. It is stored in my Treasure Chest of

Memories. Tragically, she suffered a heart attack soon afterwards. I missed her badly, the love and support she had given so freely have remained with me through the years. I look back with gratitude and appreciation for her kindness when I needed it most.

Karen soon became aware that she was the only one of her friends who lived in an apartment, and cries of, "Why can't we live in a house like everyone else", echoed in my ears. Being hesitant to make a promise I would be unable to fulfil, I only answered with "One day we will have a house and a car", whilst simultaneously sending a silent request to the Universe that these gifts would be granted. A seed of an idea took root, grew and blossomed. I canvassed the real estate agents for something within my financial ability, close to shops, bus and schools. So it was, the miracle appeared. As I left the market with my weekly grocery supplies, this lovely real estate salesman stopped me and said, "I have a house for you, when can you view it?" I could have hugged him.

It was old. It was dilapidated. It was perfect. It even had an open fireplace and a small garden, front and back. With the help of friends, we moved in two weeks later. The children were ecstatic. There were no arguments about helping to unpack and store our belongings. I viewed with apprehension the ancient stove and set about giving it a much needed clean. There were three bedrooms and quite an extensive sunroom at the front of the house. It had a good feel. Meanwhile, I had begun a relationship with a patron of the club where I worked. He was divorced and was good with my children. They both accepted him, which I considered of utmost importance. He was instrumental in negotiating an old station wagon for me, for which he paid a few dollars and was able to coax it into working order. We thought we were royalty, riding in a limousine. But above all, I gave thanks that the promises I had made to my children had come to pass.

In addition, I could now search for more well-paid work a little further afield. Once again, the Universe provided a miracle. Through a network of friends, I heard there was a sales position which had just become available at a publisher, 20-minutes' drive away. With hope in my heart, I set off for the interview on a sunny September morning. The work was not involved so much with sales, as with promotion and presentation of a display in the reception area. I also sold slightly damaged books to staff at a much-reduced price. The hours were nine to five, now I would need after school care for both my children. Joy. For a small fee, the kindergarten opposite the apartment where we used to live, agreed to care for them until 5:30.

I did my sums and worked out that I could just afford petrol and after-school care, plus school uniforms and all the extra demands on my income. My biggest outlay was the purchase of a small washing machine. I would manage to pay for it over three months, but I couldn't afford the delivery fee. I needed to somehow transport it to our new home in the back of my old station wagon. It was loaded for me, but how to heave it up the three steps and into the kitchen? I just had to ask the children for help. With much effort, it was done. After scraping our knuckles and receiving a sharp pain in my spine, I knew I had done some further damage.

Rest, Recover. I remembered these wise words from my long sojourn in hospital. Optimistically I thought, "tomorrow the pain will be gone." But it was not. It was worse. Again, I panicked. If I was unable to work, we would lose our home. It was then I remembered being told of a chiropractor in the nearby suburb, who "magically" eased injured spines. But how much would it cost? I considered my options. I just had to visit this Miracle worker. My mobility was critical to our survival. However, I was totally unprepared for what I saw as rather brutal adjustments. Feeling battered and sore, I left his clinic, staggered to my car and burst into tears.

To my surprise, it worked. The following day, although still sore, I could move less painfully and I sent a silent prayer of gratitude. The Universe was looking after me. Relief flooded my whole being and my spirits were once again restored. Both Karen and Kyle now approached me with pleading eyes. They wanted a kitten. Now we had a house, how could I refuse? The pet shop had a variety of kittens, all of which were cute and adorable. Which one was to be ours? I hold a belief to this day, that we are shown paths and directions in our lives and it is up to us to listen to guidance for our choices. In this instance, the decision was made by a tiny tortoiseshell female who purred quietly and licked our hands. She had chosen us.

There followed weeks of joy. She brought laughter and happiness into our lives. Long after my children were asleep, I played and cuddled her. So the deep bond of love was forged for the second time, between myself and a member of the animal kingdom. Then sorrow overtook us, she became sick from a virus which she had picked up whilst in the pet shop. I was devastated. She had had such a short life, my only consolation was that she had given and received unconditional love in our home. My promise to my equally distressed children was that she now lived in heaven and was being cared for by the angels. We could not conceive of having another kitten in the near future. Someday, when the pain of loss had eased. But not yet.

Life moved on, and I felt it was time to end the relationship I was in. Our views on life were so different. I enjoyed my work, it was my saviour in times such as this. I had social contact and friends amongst my co-workers. Another Christmas approached and I was given a sizeable financial bonus which I squirreled away in preparation to pay for child care during school holidays.

I knew we would have to move out of our home for four weeks, while the owners moved in for their beach holidays. We stashed all our belongings in one of the rooms and locked the door. I was able to take two weeks' holidays from work and booked a caravan for us at a resort a few miles further north. It was a wonderful holiday. Warm, balmy days and mild nights. I sun-baked, while the children played in the sand. We played board games in our temporary home during the evenings. Shortly after our arrival, a family with three boys and a girl moved into the next caravan. Instant friendships developed. They offered to take Kyle out with their boys during the day while Jane, their daughter, came with Karen and I.

It was a perfect arrangement for all of us. The sunny days continued and we glowed with health and wellbeing. Until one morning, as I sat outside eating breakfast, I heard a scream. It was Kyle. I knew his cry from a distance as all mothers recognise their own child's distress. He had had an unfortunate encounter with a low wire strung between two posts designed for hanging beach towels to dry. He ran home to me with an ugly welt on his neck. He calmed after he was told he was okay and still standing. He had sustained no major damage. Once more I breathed a sigh of relief and gratitude.

All too soon, our idyllic holiday was over but I felt renewed and rested. My return to my workplace posed no feelings of dread. While I carried out a stock-take at work, we spent the remaining two weeks in a local caravan park. I was able to have my children with me at work occasionally. An elderly lady from the local community was kind enough to volunteer to care for them on the remaining days. Once again we survived and thrived. Just.

With no warning, a quiet bombshell of bad news burst upon my sense of wellbeing and security. Our home was on the market. Once again, I was plunged into despair. Even though I was offered a one hundred percent mortgage, I immediately realized there was no chance I could afford the monthly repayments. Our home was sold five days later to the first family to view it. It seemed our lives were ruled by the lack of money and lack of resources to end this cycle. This had to change. I vowed we would survive this latest dilemma. But how? Again, we were blessed with a solution, our lovely real estate man approached me with an offer of an open-ended lease to care-take a project home. Although for sale, the real estate at this high end of the market was slow. I grasped the offer and duly viewed the property. It was my idea of heaven. Set on the side of a hill, with views across the water, it was quiet and secluded, and I instantly knew how wonderful this opportunity was to be.

I looked with amazement at the pool set amongst the lush but easily managed garden. What fun we would have. The children loved it. Karen had just begun senior school and the bus stop was a short walk up the hill. Our immediate neighbours were three young families, friendly and welcoming. Joyfully, we settled in. However, it wasn't long before I realised my present income wouldn't support my growing family and increased rent. Another job search. The reluctance of leaving the position I loved, needed to be pushed aside. My sales experience contributed towards securing a job with a greeting card company, with a higher wage and a company car. This almost compensated for the necessity of moving on. My perspective widened as I travelled throughout New South Wales. I was initiated into a whole new way of life. Interviewing prospective casual workers in outlying country towns entailed staying overnight away from my children. This was a huge adjustment and wrench on my part.

My new babysitter (or child-minder, as Karen was almost twelve and Kyle nine), proved to be a treasure. An older lady, with good references and a small car of her own. My confidence in her ability soared as the children declared their affection for her. Our time together proved even more precious. Young friends and their mothers visited frequently on weekends. We enjoyed exchanging thoughts and ideas while our children swam and played in the pool. This was truly my ideal secluded haven and I prayed we could live here for a few more summers. An unrealistic desire at best. In my heart, I knew this would not be so.

Nevertheless, it was a shock when I arrived home one day to find a SOLD sign posted in our driveway. With a heavy heart, I began another search. Although the home I found was in a more convenient location, it emanated dark energy. Something I could not quite fathom. However, it was my only option. The garden was small, as was the house. Somehow

I knew we would not be happy here. My joie de vivre disappeared and was replaced with a feeling of resignation.

This flowed through to my work and my children. Somehow I was unable to shake it off. Why? Surely I had a greater inner strength. Or had it all been drained from my mind and my spirit. Another change of work situation further instilled this feeling in me. My job had become unnecessary to the burgeoning company. However, I was rewarded with an excellent reference. This stood me in good stead with the first job I applied for and I was immediately hired. I scored another income increase and a prestigious company vehicle.

On top of this, I began dating a good looking business man of some note. I had been aware of his interest for some time. Also divorced, he was handsome, knowledgeable, and good company. This proved to be a salve for my increasing low mood. At this time, looking back, my sense of who I was and my divine path in this life had all but disappeared. It had certainly taken a back seat as I focussed on this new relationship and the changes in my life. We were taken to restaurants as a family and spent time with his friends.

Truth be known, they were not really "my kind of people", but the social scene beckoned. After six months he asked if I would move in with him. He had recently bought a large home nearby. His pride of ownership and elevation in status radiated strongly. It had beautiful slate grey floors and high vaulted ceilings. The wide balconies overlooked the nearby sleepy beachside suburb. The outlook was superb, stretching out to engulf a 180-degree ocean view. By all accounts a paradise, a dwelling fit for royalty. Yet it lacked a warm welcoming ambiance and I initially wondered about the history of the previous owners. I was later to find out they had been bankrupted. I had felt their desperation and their distress. Happiness would be hard to achieve here. My intuition proved to be correct. I began to smoke and to drink more alcohol than I knew was good for me. My children, although initially happy, also began to suffer, and to make matters worse, Ron had decided to visit Australia.

I shook with apprehension at the thought. In addition, many of Karen's peers had begun to smoke cigarettes and she also took up the habit. This distressed me. Maybe she would not have begun this addiction if she had not seen my habit. Guilt overwhelmed me. After Ron's visit, it was obvious he had tried to denigrate and put doubt in the children's minds as to my suitability to be their primary carer. Karen was most affected and became difficult and moody. I tried to equate this with the hormonal upheaval of her teenage years. In spite of this, I remained steadfast in my resolve to refrain from revealing their father's underlying abusive nature. There was little support from my partner. How could I blame him? It was not an easy task taking on a woman with two children. Shortly afterwards I knew it was time to leave the relationship. It just wasn't working.

With a heavy heart, I began the next search for a home. Of necessity, it needed to be almost immediate. I sighed with resignation. Our lives were fraught with the burden of multiple moves. I longed to be shown a place where we could find sustained happiness and peace. A wish too ambitious? Yes, it would be granted, but not at that time. Our next home was a ground floor, small but adequate, three-bedroom apartment. Its redeeming factors were the view across the valley to the water and it was within walking distance of public transport and shops. An opportunity for extra income had presented itself in the form of promotional work involving occasional evenings.

Karen was now fifteen and Kyle twelve. I needed to provide ongoing costly uniforms, school books, and outings as well as sporting equipment. Kyle was passionate about baseball and cricket. At times life seemed a long unending struggle to provide the necessary essentials for our lives. My determination to survive and optimism for the future were often at a low ebb. The harder I tried to move forward, the more the Universe appeared to place blocks to my progress. My life was filled with ever mounting things waiting to be done and "me time" was none existent. I fell into bed each night exhausted in mind, body and spirit. Where would my path lead me?

However, shortly after we moved in, I began to hear a noise outside my bedroom window during the evening and discovered a small black cat sitting on the window ledge outside. She looked up pleadingly at me, but I knew we weren't allowed to have pets in this home. She persisted night after night and eventually she appeared at the front door during the day. I found it impossible to resist giving her a saucer of milk. Although not malnourished she looked thin and seemed lost and alone.

A search for her owners began. I enquired around the area and even put an advertisement in the local shops. I felt there would be no response and I was correct. No-one came forward. I realised this was the second cat who had adopted us, and at a time which was difficult not only for me but for Karen also. I pronounced she had been sent as a gift to help uplift us both. How right I was, for she brought so much joy and laughter into all our lives for the ensuing period of almost fifteen years.

Love and miracles

Hugh

Unconditional love is all that matters.

What did the Universe have in store for me? Just at this time when I was so vulnerable, a miracle began to unfold, although at the time I didn't see it as such. My dear friend Pat, from our time at the apartment, had been aware of my unhappiness over recent events. She invited me to go to a weekly get together. She encouraged me, saying most were singles and there would be music and dancing. This news sparked my interest but I didn't feel ready to rejoin the social scene. However, a few weeks later, I was determined to make the effort with this new social venture. I realised how much I had missed sharing conversation and experiences with like-minded people. In addition, the thought of uplifting music and the opportunity to dance drew me like a magnet.

I loved it. There was no pressure to form a partnership with anyone, rather to relax and enjoy. I was hooked. I met new and interesting people, both men and women from many walks of life. Amongst them was Hugh. He was Scottish. Though not tall, in fact quite short in stature, he had a charismatic personality. Glasses and a beard set him apart from other men of his age group. I was later to discover he was seven years my junior. Yikes. I watched as he danced, attracting admiring glances from some of the ladies. He rarely left the dance floor extending an invitation to each lady in turn.

I found his conversation intriguing, but the one attribute which attracted me beyond all other was his ability to listen. This was a quality I had rarely found in my experiences with the male species. Having discovered we lived in the same suburb, he offered to drive me each week to the gathering. This gave us time to talk and we found we had much in common. Divorced, with no children of his own, he began to visit while I was getting ready for the outing. He soon connected with Karen and Kyle. This developing friendship continued to flourish for six months. Though not a romantic relationship, it was a solid foundation upon which to build.

At about this time, when Hugh and I were becoming good friends, my mother was working on persuading my father to visit the children and I. I later discovered it had taken two years and her success only came to pass after accusing him of not wanting to ever see his daughter and grandchildren again. She wisely knew I had neither the means or the time financially to make the long trip. I would still need to pay rent while I was away and would almost certainly have lost my job at that time. They arrived on a mild August morning, tired and travel weary. My heart was pounding after the long wait at the airport. The anticipation of finally connecting with my mother once more caused both excitement and trepidation. How would my father react? Our relationship was strained at the best of times.

My fears were in part unfounded. I was greeted with a hug and an acknowledgement of kinship, which was all I could have expected at that time. How good it was to see my mother, older but still steadfast and strong at almost 70 years old. I had obtained permission to work a three-day week with a full week's holiday during the second week of their visit. This was ostensibly so they could recover from their flight. It would also give us time to talk and allow them to renew their relationship with Karen, who was now 16, and Kyle, who was 13. I had surrendered my bedroom and slept in the lounge room on a borrowed camp bed. It proved a successful strategy to a point. Kyle was polite and chatty. Karen was at times verging on rudeness, which mum shrugged off as the terrible teens. How wise she was, to have the ability to dissipate any bad feelings with this simple sentence.

We planned a trip to Queensland during my week's holiday. We stopped half way for an overnight stay at a coastal caravan resort near Coffs Harbour. It took some persuading as my father had an aversion to caravans. However, the one I had booked had an ensuite and shower and this won him over. We stopped frequently on the way to stretch our legs and enjoy sandwiches and tea from our thermos flasks while admiring the scenery. The open countryside and the forests gave way to banana plantations and further north, extensive sugar cane plantations.

We arrived at the caravan resort in the late afternoon. It was a perfect choice, with the beach a short stroll through tropical palms. Tree ferns as tall as two-story buildings opened out to pristine white sand and sparkling water. I was overjoyed, running and laughing, happy and free. The following morning, we set off again. After a full day's travel, we arrived at our destination. The apartment was spacious, light and clean and met with my father's approval, much to my relief.

Mild and sunny days followed. My parents rested and recovered. I soaked up the sun, revelling in the opportunity to enjoy this time of rejuvenation. It was a release from the stresses of my working week and juggling my wage to pay the rent, our food, and other living expenses. I booked a day out to a nearby island, a short boat ride away. The trip included a Hawaiian barbeque and time to explore its caves and waterways. Another delightful outing to a sea life centre with dolphins, coral fish, and rides for the children, proved a success and gave both my parents the experience of the diversity of Australian wildlife. I cooked our evening meals, endeavouring to include local fruit and vegetables that were often in short supply in the UK stores.

All too soon the time came for them to leave, early in September before our days became too warm. In addition, my mother loved this autumn month in the UK. It's promise of misty mornings and clear days enticed her home to enjoy "the season of mists and mellow fruitfulness." I hugged mum with tears in my eyes and gained an unexpected hug from my father as well. I was grateful for his willingness to pay for our holiday and share food and other expenses along the way. However, I didn't feel this was the last time I would see them both.

Christmas came and went. I was happy, my social life had blossomed and both my children were settled at school. However, it was New Year's Day that would change my life forever. One of our group offered to host a New Year's party at his home overlooking the harbour. The wine flowed freely and the conversation was animated, but it was his budgerigar's antics which attracted my attention. I stood fascinated and when I looked up, there was Hugh. Our eyes met and we both burst into fits of laughter. I discovered humour in that moment and my heart opened to receive this gift with soaring excitement and joy. This was the spark which ignited what was to be a life-long romance.

Several months later, Hugh proposed. It felt so right, even though I had asked for time to think about it. We made the trip to the jewellers and chose a beautiful diamond cluster ring. I went home to make the announcement to Karen and Kyle. I knew both of my children, who were now young adults, were aware of this close relationship that was scarcely hidden from them. However, Karen's reaction was swift and angry. She wasn't open to the news. She totally rejected the idea of my second marriage, although she liked Hugh as a friend. I was devastated. My hopes for a future filled with new found happiness and family harmony fell apart and scattered on the ground.

How would I overcome this seemingly impossible hurdle? I was reassured by the thought that she would accept this news given time. Hugh was patient and understanding. We shared a close mental, emotional and spiritual bond, surely nothing could tear us apart. Time passed. I wore my precious ring on a gold chain next to my heart, not revealing our engagement to our friends at this time. Emotions settled and as we continued attending social functions, eventually our obvious connection was brought into the open. It was as though a precious jewel had been discovered hidden in a casket. An engagement party was secretly planned by my friend Ann and sprung upon us as a wonderful surprise. So a wedding date was set, but meanwhile, we resolved not to live together.

I began to look for a new home for us. Hugh was overseas when I found it - or rather the Universe presented it. I felt uplifted, blessed and energised once more. My life path was on track with this new beginning. I knew we would travel our path together in alignment with one another and with universal guidance and protection. I was later to discover Hugh had felt the presence of an elderly female spirit virtually all his life, watching over him. He felt she was a guardian angel or ancestor. As our closeness had developed she had left, knowing she would no longer be needed. Having been told of this event, I experienced an overwhelming sense of gratitude and realisation that we had been guided to meet. This relationship was meant to be and had been blessed both in this lifetime and those we were yet to have.

Our new home was old, but with an expansive view over the surrounding suburbs and the ocean and extending to the shimmering horizon on which the city stood. I knew the increased rent would prove a struggle until the date we had chosen for our wedding. Hugh was saving for the associated cost of the wedding and for our honeymoon. Having initially chosen Fiji as our destination, I discovered an island off the coast of Queensland. A jewel set in the sparkling coral sea with abundant wildlife. There were coastal walks and bushwalks. The comfortable, resort style accommodation beckoned me. I had visited the island with my dear friend Pat and my children and had fallen in love with its wild, almost deserted beaches, stunning lookouts, and friendly locals. I knew instinctively that Hugh would like it.

Even though I knew our union was "made in heaven", as the day approached, I grew more nervous. This was a huge step for me, indeed for both of us. All the arrangements were made. Kyle was to give me away and Karen was my only bridesmaid. Thankfully she seemed happier about my impending marriage.

$\mathcal{H}$armony restored

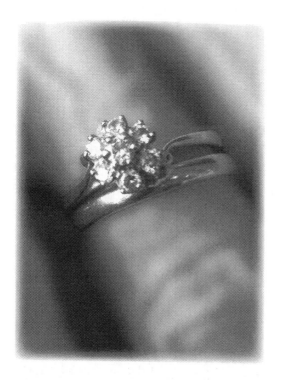

*Breathtaking moments to last a lifetime will
arrive when your need is greatest.*

Hugh had been so patient with Karen. He made a huge effort to help
and reassure her of his friendship, no matter what. This is a gift I have
been constantly grateful for. The day arrived, hot and sunny. Our life
together was about to begin. With mounting excitement and shaking
hands, I piled my hair on top of my head, in a style I seldom wore. I

donned the beautiful lace trimmed, cream dress that my dear friend Ann had so lovingly made and applied a little makeup.

Finally, we bade farewell to our guests after a day of laughter, happiness, speeches and toasts to our future. My happiness literally shone like a golden aura. I was blessed indeed. As I had felt, Hugh also loved our island retreat. In fact, we continued to spend many wonderful holidays there, walking, singing and dancing on the beaches, rain or shine and exploring the variety of bush walks. We marvelled at the diversity of wildlife. Birds we had never seen soared above us. Wallabies grazed in the bush as we walked past and turtles delighted and enhanced our love of nature. Huge pods of dolphins surfed through the waves, taking our breath away in admiration and wonderment at their skill.

We were so enamoured by this idyllic lifestyle and each other's company. It was on one such holiday, a few years later, that I recalled the third lesson from my last life. While I was swimming in the sparkling crystal clear water, I suddenly looked up to see an eagle circling above me. Soaring in an upward vortex of air, majestic and serene, "Fly with the Eagles, far above the squabbling crows who may taunt and tease, and try to bring you down."

Returning to reality arrived too soon. With a jolt to our senses, the period of Hugh's integration into our family unit proved more challenging than either of us had anticipated. I found the extra workload overwhelming on top of my demanding job, and at one point dissolved into tears. Too much to do, too little time. As always, Hugh was supportive and took on some of the household tasks, while admitting he felt "like an orange in a lemon factory." This admission brought back the laughter and we quickly returned to perfect harmony. My children became adjusted to, and accepting of, my marriage. Over time, Karen grew to consider Hugh as her father figure.

About a year into our marriage, as we became more stable, I realised that I could now branch out in my business life. I had some valuable contacts and offers of public relations work in the areas of health and tourism. After discussing my thoughts of a freelance career with Hugh and finding him supportive and encouraging, I consulted my intuitive nature. My insight came to me clearly with a message to go ahead. There followed several years of interesting, varied and at times, stressful work, which involved a certain amount of travel within Australia.

I loved seeing new environments, especially the islands off the coast of North Queensland. Their beauty inspired and rejuvenated me. I loved the remoteness and the proximity to diverse wildlife, whilst I was liaising with international journalists, photographers and resort staff. The health side of my business prospered, as did the financial advice I was now qualified to give to joint venture participants. I now realised I was earning a substantial income, but as time moved on, I felt a certain lack of connection with my life purpose. I began to turn towards a more holistic and spiritual path.

Having seen disease and illness among my work colleagues, I was drawn to healing modalities and began to study Reiki, attaining Reiki Master certification. This shift brought peace and personal gratification, knowing I was helping others with the healing energy I was able to channel. Advising on wellness and a healthy lifestyle now beckoned me. I researched information on courses that could teach me to help those who are open to a new and healthier lifestyle. One in which they can maintain vibrant wellness at any age. I studied two online courses, first for energy healing, and then a more advanced level of life coaching. I was overjoyed to gain these qualifications.

We lived in this home for five years, during which time, Karen met and fell in love with her future husband. A few months into their relationship, they moved into an apartment in a nearby suburb. When I entered her empty room I experienced the "empty nest syndrome." I missed her presence so badly I felt a physical pain, that of heartache. My first born child had left, never to return to our family home. Twelve months later they were married. Karen looking stunning, her shining golden hair cascading to her waist, her eyes glowing with the happiness I had always dreamed would be hers. Her new husband Chris, handsome, proud and nervous by her side as they left for their honeymoon.

Meanwhile, we had moved once more, to a home we were to occupy for eleven years. I longed to be able to buy a home in this beachside area we both loved, but our age and financial status prohibited this. Over time I became reconciled to the fact that this might not happen, and the burning ambition subsided.

China and beyond

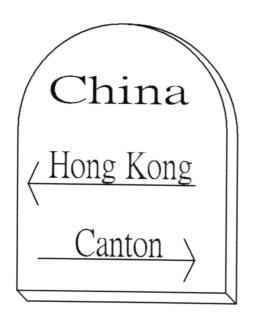

Daydreams are a manifestation of the soul's desires.

My work continued to prosper. One of my colleagues who had contacts in the Chinese pharmaceutical industry suggested a visit to China. The aim was to negotiate importation of the herbal remedies I had become so passionate about. This was initially on a small scale, with the intention of testing the Australian market. The concept grabbed my interest and having borrowed some capital I prepared for this trip. I based myself in Hong Kong and scheduled meetings with three CEO's in Guangzhou (Canton). A guide and chaperone were assigned to accompany me and we met at the train station early on the second day of my visit.

Mr. Chou was eighty plus years old and spoke little English, but I felt safe and confident in his presence. He had a wife and teenage daughter in Canton which was the second reason for this trip. Not surprisingly, I was the only non-Chinese passenger in the overcrowded carriages. However, I enjoyed the journey, travelling past rice paddies with yaks and straw-hatted farmers working in the fields. In the hazy distance were majestic, affluent looking homes resting on the slopes as though presiding over their domain.

On reaching Canton, I was astonished to see there was very little vehicular traffic but an abundance of bicycles thronged the streets. Most had one or two small children either sitting behind or in front of their parent, entrancing me with their wide enquiring eyes. My visits to the pharmaceutical laboratories and factories were eye opening. The pristine cleanliness of the workplace and the workers' competence impressed me and remains in my memory to this day. I was plied with samples and literature, which I accepted with gratitude from these honest and welcoming people.

That evening, I was introduced to Mr. Chou's wife, who spoke not a word of English but delighted me with her hospitality. She attempted to teach me a few words of Mandarin, which have long since escaped my memory. I found the food she had prepared to be delicious and although so different to my normal diet was accepted by my sensitive digestion. In fact, because I sought out only food consumed by the residents, I avoided suffering the digestive distress experienced by fellow westerners.

On leaving Canton, Mr. Chou gave me a photo of his daughter and asked if I would find a Chinese Australian husband for her, in return for his having accompanied me. A task which I accepted gracefully but secretly without much confidence of success. Mr. Chou planned to stay in Canton for another week, so my return to Hong Kong was alone on the equally crowded train. As we left the station, many people spotted the empty seat beside me, but having seen I was not only a woman but a woman on her own, none would occupy it. Their culture was so different from the western way of life.

After two more days in Hong Kong, I felt anxious to return home but grateful for the learning experiences and the exposure to this ancient and powerful land. My friend Moira knew of a Chinese family and with relief, I was able to send a photograph and contact address of a suitable young man for Mr. Chou's daughter. However, I was not privy to the outcome of this introduction. Neither did my business contacts produce an ongoing import/export situation.

Psychic connection

*A calming meditation practice and time in nature can
enable anyone to increase their inner knowing.*

Around this time, the Universe sparked my interest in developing my
psychic ability. I scanned the local advertisements for workshops and
courses and soon came across a small notice which literally leapt from
the page towards me. My life was about to change dramatically and I
knew instinctively there would be no going back. Our initial meeting

at her home came as a complete surprise. I had imagined her to look a certain way, maybe a small, slim woman with colourful flowing cotton skirts, such as a gypsy woman might wear. However, this was not so. Her expression was such that she must have seen the astonishment on my face. Her name was Helen. Tall, well built and wearing lashings of bright blue eye shadow and a purple track suit with playing card motifs on the front.

The energy emanating from her was almost overpowering, her brilliant blue eyes appeared to have the ability to see into my very soul. After Helen had outlined the basis of the course, I asked where she had acquired her knowledge. She responded immediately stating, "I have lived it." Intuitively, I knew this to be true and I signed up for the workshops. A huge learning curve, increased psychic ability, connection to the universe and spiritual experiences followed. I began to see auras and I joyfully practised this new gift. I often sensed spirits around me. Proof of their presence appeared in the photos we took of our new grandchild, Lucy. A tiny spirit appeared as a bright spark.

I loved to lie on my hammock in the garden during the afternoon and it was at this time that nanna's spirit came to visit me and chatted about her family, my mother, and uncle. I had long since realised Keith was her favourite. Mum knew it too, but it made no difference to her love for him and her mother. In fact, she was the one who looked after nanna during the times she was ill, as daughters often do.

As my intuition and psychic abilities increased I began to have many paranormal experiences. Initially, I would see spirit beings, ranging from people I had known in this life, to Angels and Guides assigned to help those I met in my day to day work or recreational time. I also became aware of alien beings observing me intently, though in a non-interfering capacity. One such being, appeared in our kitchen as I was preparing lunch one day. He (for it seemed to be a masculine energy) was tall and slim with a face not unlike a human and wore a pale beige tunic and pants.

However, one night I was actually taken by a group of aliens who looked totally different, more alike to the traditional portrayal we see in the movies. I found myself in a bright metallic room without windows which I associated with an operating theatre. I realised that although I was not physically constrained in any way, I was unable to move. There were five in all, with the one who was in charge beginning to point to various areas of my body, communicating not with speech but with a mind connection or intuition. I knew he was analysing me as a mature human specimen and passing his observations to his students. This appeared to happen over an extended time span, but looking back, I saw it was a matter of only a few minutes.

I was returned to our home unharmed, though somewhat stunned and disoriented. It took some time before I could move freely once more. I rose a little groggily and cleansed my aura, as I had been taught by Helen. This abduction was soon followed with what I call night visitors. They ranged from my mother, my Guardian Angel, my friend's father (who checked on me to see if I was ok), to several spirits who needed help to move on.

Kyle heard his name being called one night and I resolved to find the history of the owners of this home. A neighbour revealed that their young son had collapsed and died there. Sadness for the family enveloped me. I was lying in our garden, relaxing in my hammock one warm afternoon, when he came and sat on the grass beside me, weeping and saying "They have all gone away and left me." Helen had taught me how to help spirits who are in shock from a sudden unexpected death, who were caught between this world and the next. I spoke quietly to him, following Helen's insight, I informed him that his father, who had had also passed on, was waiting for him and directed him to look over his left shoulder. I saw him walk towards the Light. It was one of the most moving and emotional experiences I have ever had.

Following this, I found I was able to channel information from various guides and spirits and was introduced to my personal guide, Amon. He was tall and slim and wore a brown hooded robe. I first saw him as a herbalist. In any event, he had a good knowledge of herbs. Softly spoken, but with a strong and all seeing energy, he was able to perceive my thoughts and life direction at an incredibly deep level. He was perfect for me and my developing psychic abilities. He was to remain with me for several years and I had a great love for him. My meditations grew in intensity and information literally poured into my mind. I began to journal daily. My dreams became more vivid and I was given the ability to source their meaning and their messages. I now found it increasingly difficult to balance my spiritual life and my everyday existence.

Hugh was unendingly understanding and willing to listen to the encounters I felt able to share. How I looked forward to Helen's weekly workshops, where I continued to learn alongside other like-minded attendees. I made new friends amongst the group, one of which endures to this day. The sharing of our mutual experiences proved invaluable. I learned of alien beings. I was taken, while meditating, to a planet way beyond our galaxy. I saw the inhabitants, tall and slim, gathering crops in the fertile fields. Their peace and ability to be in tune with their environment drew me towards them. They had learned from their past mistakes where mismanagement had destroyed their home planet.

The first acknowledgement of the gift I was to receive came in a message from Amon *"You will be given a gift. You DO deserve it. My purpose is to teach you. I ask nothing in return. I will stay as long as is needed. You will become a wise woman and will help and advise many people. They will come to you, not only for healing but for comfort and to be near you."* The truth was, I did not feel worthy or deserving of these gifts. Looking back on my life I only focused on my mistakes, misdeeds, and dark thoughts. At this point I found them distressing as never before. I pleaded for forgiveness and vowed to begin anew on my journey in this lifetime. My friendship with Helen grew and we spent increasing time together. She had a raucous sense of humour. We laughed at the synchronicities in our lives and cried over the destruction which was becoming increasingly evident on our beautiful planet.

Changes

*Life is all about change, good or bad. Being open to its challenges
enables us to move forward on our divine life path.*

Shortly before the turn of the century, we needed to move once more.
My first response was distress. The thought of another upheaval
overwhelmed me. However, it had to be. Luckily (except nothing
happens by luck), a perfect potential home presented itself. It nestled
on the side of a hill, with views over the valley to the ocean. We all loved

it at first sight. It's energy and vibration reached out and captivated me, prompting me to ask for information on its history. I was told, "this house has been loved for twenty-five years." I felt the love had been so well absorbed into the very fabric of the structure, that it literally radiated through the air. We signed the lease that day. Kyle had asked for the large room for himself on the lower level which had its own entry and bathroom area. The rent was only affordable because of our three incomes. Happiness and optimism overtook me as we began packing our belongings in preparation. In no time we were once more settled and I hugged this new experience of security and contentment to me.

Despite the distance which separated us, my mother's frequent letters kept us in close contact. She wrote an attention catching letter. It felt as though she was having a conversation with me. I attempted to emulate this gift, although somewhat unsuccessfully. She had often asked if I would make the long trip to visit her. Initially, I resisted. The thought of the cost and the long flight put me off. However, Hugh encouraged me. Wisely reminding me that she and my father were now in their eighties and this may be my last chance. To my surprise, Kyle said he would like to go as well. So it was settled. However, Kyle, although keen to board the aircraft, hadn't fully understood the length of the flight. After two hours he was ready to disembark. Having been informed we were still flying over Australia he became resigned to the long, tiring journey. I had booked a short overnight stopover in Singapore which was a lifesaver for us both.

John and his wife Ann met us at Heathrow airport in London on a rainy afternoon. We stayed with them for a few days. The beauty of the English countryside in the summer sunshine once more endeared itself to me. It was wonderful to renew my connection with John and his family. Kyle, now thirty years old, had little memory of his English heritage and the country of his birth. He enjoyed visiting various places of interest. motor museums, ancient castles and all things masculine. I delighted in the gardens that were frequently open to the public. I had two powerful spirit guides especially allocated to me at this time, Ezra and Hiawatha. Their strength and guidance sustained me. Keith, the uncle I had adored since childhood, immediately told me "you have two very powerful guides." I could only nod, and acknowledge his insight, while Kyle looked on with curiosity, as I had not shared this information with him. I sought peaceful areas to meditate, amongst the natural surroundings. Ezra guided me away from areas which were unsafe.

In spite of my reluctance to embark on this trip, once there, I had the most wonderful time. My guides were constantly with me, giving me encouragement and support. This was my first visit to John and Ann's home in Surrey. I loved the ambiance and warm loving vibration it provided. The typically English garden, with fold up canvas deck chairs that appeared on sunny days, completed my happiness. Their lifestyle appeared relaxed, yet vibrant with energy. I appreciated the few days that we spent there. Being introduced to the local area and nearby country town was a joy. I walked to the shopping centre via a pathway that wound past vegetable allotments and the rear gardens of country homes. They were only visible through small gaps in their fences. This gave me a further insight into the energy of the area. I loved to browse through the quaint antique shops and call in for a tasty afternoon tea at one of the cafés.

All too soon our visit came to an end. Roy arrived to take us to mum and dad's home, where a warm welcome awaited. Mum was animated and excited to see us. She plied us with warm hugs, a hot lunch, and exchange of latest family news. My father, who now had diabetes, was partially disabled after suffering a stroke. Time with mum was precious and I was overjoyed to have made the decision to visit. I was keen to show Kyle the surrounding area and the house where I spent my childhood, a short drive away.

My father allowed me to drive his car. Although he could no longer drive, he was unwilling to sell his beloved car. Thus followed trips to Litchfield and a walk around the cathedral there, which left Kyle amazed at its grandeur and size. We also enjoyed a day at Warwick

Castle with Roy and his family. As I stood in the grassy courtyard, I vividly recalled being in the exact same spot as a young teenager with my best friend Elisabeth on a rare school outing. Many years had passed but little had changed in this place, whereas major changes had occurred in my life.

A day with mum and dad at my cousin Lorraine's home in the beautiful Cotswolds was a joy, although I felt dad's tension with regard to the safety of his vehicle. How I enjoyed seeing the country pub with its low wooden beams. The horse brasses adorning the walls and the horse drawn wagon delivering beer barrels, so much a part of country life. This was followed by a delicious lunch that Lorraine had prepared for us. It was a special day and held happy memories that I have stored in the Treasure Chest of my Mind.

My birthplace had encompassed many changes over the years. Vandals and petty criminals, intent on causing harm, were abundant but not always in evidence. In spite of this, I felt protected and at peace, enjoying what was to be my last visit with both parents in this lifetime. At this stage, I had not yet found peace with my father's behaviour, but maintained a pleasant enough flow of conversation. The visit was over too soon and as I hugged mum, my tears began to flow, both in gratitude and sorrow for the difficult life path she had chosen. I had gained so much wisdom as a child, her kindness and steadfast personality had inspired and sustained me. I remain forever grateful and honoured to be her child. Kyle decided to stay for a further month or two, travelling with Keith to his villa in the south of France, while I prepared to return to Australia. I was missing Hugh and the wide blue skies of my adopted homeland. I knew this would be the last time I would see both of my parents in this life, so it was with ill-concealed emotion that I bade them farewell.

I had booked a two-day stopover in Singapore to experience the culture and re-adjust to the similar time zone. Singapore was just three hours behind Australia's east coast. My first impression was the airport's cleanliness as was found throughout Singapore, even in the city streets, not a sign of litter was to be seen. My hotel was on Sentosa Island, where I was shown to a huge room overlooking an equally huge pool which was in fact, more akin to a lagoon. My first priority was to unpack, change into my swimming costume and enjoy a relaxing hour, swimming and lazing by the pool. Heaven. After a refreshing shower, an early evening meal beckoned.

The resort restaurant looked inviting. I changed into a full-length skirt and blouse, suitable for this occasion. On venturing in, I discovered it to be delightfully cool, welcoming and totally empty of diners. Journal in hand, I ordered a glass of wine and a meal. I proceeded to enter into my journal my thoughts of the day. I wrote of new experiences, cultures, and customs. Having consumed the delicious meal, I saw the chef approach my table. Smiling, he introduced himself and commented on my choice of a side dish of green chillies. Apparently, this was a taste few customers of the western culture indulged in. However, it was one which my palate found intensely enjoyable. I experienced two more days of discovery and exploration, including a mandatory coffee at the famous Raffles restaurant. It was enough to stimulate my interest in international travel in the future. However, the Universe and future events decreed it was not to be.

$\mathcal{D}$espair and joy

Good health and happiness are two of life's greatest gifts.

We had a happy welcome home gathering for Kyle when he returned. He had remained in England for a further three months, returning home when the English autumn became too cold. However, his health was about to have a downwards spiral. Six months later, he became ill with bronchitis and was hospitalised with pneumonia. His health then deteriorated to such an extent, that he was unable to work. Despite visits to various specialists, including traditional Chinese treatments which did help for a short while, nothing we tried was the complete answer. He became depressed and remained in his room for days curled on his bed under the doona. He had lost a third of his body weight, which shocked and disturbed me. I became increasingly concerned about both his physical and mental health.

I spoke at length with his doctor. I pleaded with the Universe for an answer, a solution. On each step that I took down the fourteen stairs to his room, I asked for the words which would help relieve his depression and suicidal thoughts. My urgent requests were always answered. I spoke the words that were given to me, words of comfort and encouragement that I would never have conceived. I believe they were more than enough to help lift and dissipate the dark thoughts and depression which haunted his mind. His doctor finally suggested he speak to a psychologist. During the consultation, the solution emerged, upon which I was so overwhelmed with gratitude, I could have hugged him. A chemical imbalance easily corrected over time with medication. Relief flooded through my whole being and I drove home with a light heart and a huge smile, hardly able to wait to tell Hugh the good news.

Very slowly, a day at a time, improvement began to emerge and within a few months, Kyle was able to return to work, albeit initially part time. My happiness and contentment returned. For a while. I phoned my mother on a weekly basis, knowing her time in this life was coming to an end. However, my last call shocked me to my very core. She had virtually lost her power of speech and found difficulty putting together a sentence, let alone a conversation. I entreated my father to call her doctor immediately, whereupon he told me she hadn't been eating or drinking and had lost a lot of weight. Her body was severely dehydrated, thus her confusion.

She was hospitalised and given fluids and various drugs to help revive her. This was unsuccessful and she passed on five days later. Although I grieved for her passing, I now realise it was her choice to leave at that time. She had done her best to nurture and bring up her three children.

Encouraging and supporting us with all the love and the knowledge she had access to. I will remain forever grateful to have been blessed with her as my mother. My father struggled on for a further two years. He became bedridden and dependent on my brother Roy and sister-in-law Liz for daily care. His mind remained clear and I continued to call each week, but I wasn't able to come to terms with his behaviour until much later. After his passing I realised I was the matriarch of the family and as such was given the honour of keeping in regular contact with my brothers and their children. A task which I found both pleasurable and rewarding.

Kyle began his first romance with a girl called Belinda who was an employee at his workplace. His euphoria was apparent. His face glowed from this new found relationship and I knew this was to be a new beginning for him. Soon they both decided to relocate to Queensland with a promise of work and a new life. None of the previous "empty nest" feeling this time for me. I was happy for this turn of events in his life. I looked forward to sharing my home, for the first time, alone with Hugh.

Three years later, they planned their wedding in the perfect setting of a botanical garden on a November afternoon. Hugh planned to drive to the wedding venue in Hervey Bay, a distance of over a 1000 Kilometres, while I, Karen and her family flew with the minimum of luggage. However, after only travelling half way there, Hugh was involved in an accident. Another car veered into his lane and spun his small van 180 degrees with major damage to the driver's side. Hugh escaped with minor facial injuries and a gash to his torso. His glasses and mobile phone were flung from the vehicle. Our luggage was damaged beyond repair but amazingly the outfits we had planned for the wedding remained intact.

It wasn't until he rang from the local hospital that I was informed of this accident. I was distraught beyond belief but filled with gratitude for both his survival and minor injuries. Hugh's cousin quickly offered to make the trip from Brisbane and to drive Hugh to the resort we had booked. Our reunion was emotional and relief flooded my mind. The day dawned, warm and sunny, how happy they both looked. I was overjoyed. Hugh and I spent a wonderful five days exploring the area, meeting other guests and forging new friendships. We returned home feeling happy and relaxed.

$\mathcal{D}$esperation

*The dawn which follows the darkest night
is always the most breathtaking.*

The following year we again planned to visit the island retreat we both loved, however as the time approached for our departure, I began to experience severe lower spinal pain. This was worse than I could remember since the car accident many years ago. I was referred for an x-ray, which revealed a further fracture in one of the same vertebrae as before. Distress overwhelmed me, not only for the pain but the inevitable cancellation of our much-anticipated trip. I realised that this time, it would take longer to heal as I was so much older. The first question for the Universe was "why has this happened?" I searched for an answer, but none came. I had a good diet, exercised regularly, and slept well. The only physical or emotional cause was the stress and anxiety I had frequently experienced. Maybe this had affected my skeletal structure.

Little did I know that a much bigger lesson had been sent. My experience had given me the most wonderful spiritual gift of wisdom and empathy that would later help me in my work. But that would be a matter of years into the future. My mobility was severely restricted. I really missed my regular visits to the local swimming pool and the friends I had made there. I could no longer enjoy evening walks with Hugh, and to my increasing distress, I then suffered two more fractures. My spine was collapsing.

My doctor referred me to a specialist, and struggling to her rooms I was told that an operation would help restore and strengthen my spine. At this stage, I would have agreed to anything to help with the pain. But it was not a success and more fractures appeared. I was in hospital once more and given morphine. Although it brought relief from the unrelenting agony, it also reduced me to a state of continual mind fog. I slept as if in a coma. Family and friends came to visit and I managed a weak smile and some sort of conversation. Hugh visited every day, his face drawn with anxiety over my weakened state and not knowing my long term prognosis.

After a few days, I resolved to convince the doctors I could manage in my home environment. I was convinced my healing would escalate once I was enfolded in the loving energies of our home. It was agreed that if I could walk along the passageway and up a short flight of stairs using a walking frame, I would be allowed to go home. I literally gritted my teeth determined to succeed with this small endeavour. Then began seven slow years of recovery. During the first six months, I could only move painfully from our bedroom to the living area and kitchen. I was still on morphine and would be for twelve more months. This was a time of extreme distress. I grieved for my mobility and the fitness I had enjoyed. I missed the social interaction as I swam and exercised at the local swim centre and I missed the balmy, moonlit walks with Hugh. I also missed the freelance PR work which I had found both challenging and inspirational. Yet I never questioned the Universe. I knew intuitively I would be shown the reason when the time was right. Meanwhile, my task was to recover and recover I would.

I was seldom reduced to tears. In fact, I only recall the one time when I heard a favourite song which brought back special memories that had been stored in the Treasure Chest of my Mind. I sobbed and let the tears flow freely. Helen was, as always, a steadfast and constant comfort and encouraged me with her insights and her sense of fun in all situations. We spent many hours speaking on the phone as she had moved from her home close by to a small property north of our area.

I was living from minute to minute, not knowing what lay ahead. Then help was presented in the form of a small article describing the work of Medical Intuitive Healers. The words leapt from the page and I researched to source one who I felt could bring my weakened body back to strength and wellness. The thought of distant healing was infinitely appealing. I immediately felt a connection with the international healer I had chosen, considering myself blessed to have sufficient funds to pay for the sessions. Although improvement took a matter of months, I began to experience less pain over time and the return of some of my strength.

My spirits lifted once again, with Hugh's continual help. He sometimes even helped me to get dressed and at my worst helped me out of bed. I knew without any doubt, that eventually I would be completely healed. After six months the next hurdle was attempting the steps to our front door and then to the garden. Gripping the handrail and with a walking stick in the other hand, I completed this momentous task under Hugh's watchful eye. How good it was to feel the gentle breeze in my hair and the sun on my face.

A few steps around our small garden with the earth beneath my feet was nectar to my soul. Joy overcame me. My next challenge was to rediscover my driving skills. I had no memory of where the controls were, thanks to the strong painkillers which had disrupted my thinking so badly and the length of time that had passed. Once mastered, the challenge was to drive the short distance to our favourite beach. Propped up with cushions, I took off. This proved easier than I had contemplated. I revelled in the wonderful energy of this special place, the sparkling ocean and the sand between my toes, restored my well-being and contentment. The sense of achievement almost took my breath away and I now looked forward to this small but important outing each day. Meeting new people at the beach café opened my mind. My communication and connection both with Mother Nature and other like-minded souls skyrocketed. I knew good things awaited me and I grew restless with anticipation.

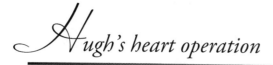Hugh's heart operation

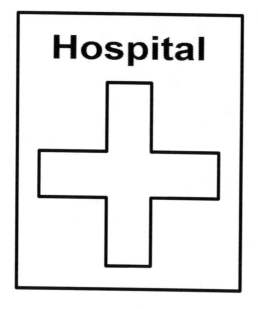

Don't do your best, if you can do better.

I had known of Hugh's vulnerability but wasn't aware at this time that he had a heart problem, a potentially serious one. We were first made aware of it after a simple doctor's visit revealed an inconsistency with its rhythm. This is known as heart arrhythmia. A heart stress test followed then an angiogram. At this stage, we thought it could be managed with medication, or worst case scenario, the insertion of a stent. This is a balloon-like addition designed to open up the offending artery.

It was not to be. Hugh arrived home from the angiogram with bad news. I immediately saw it in his expression - a heart bypass. Shock radiated outward from my inner being. This was a life-threatening operation. Over the years his arteries had become congested. This was partly due to poor dietary choices and lack of self-care (as is the case for many males), and in part inherited from both his parents.

The date was set. My children were a wonderful support for both Hugh and I. Their concern and thoughtfulness helped us through these stressful days. Kyle offered to stay with me during the week of Hugh's hospitalisation. This in itself lifted my spirit in gratitude and appreciation. Hugh had specifically asked me not to visit, he felt it would be too overwhelming to see him surrounded by tubes and equipment. I prayed – Please don't take him. Although I instinctively knew this wasn't his time to depart this life, I was nonetheless anxious. I sent, as well as asked for, healing energy both to Hugh and his surgeon.

Hugh later told me he listened continually to the relaxing meditations I had recorded and how they had helped him to remain calm during the evening before the operation. The day arrived. Karen, Kyle and I spent the endless waiting hours together. Trying to make light-hearted conversation on any subject. Much to our relief we were told he had come through the operation successfully and we were able to enjoy a restful sleep that night.

Hugh's determination to recover without setbacks both astonished and delighted me. His steadfastness and stubbornness in all things surfaced for his ultimate benefit. He refused to have visitors during the week following his operation in order to focus solely on his recovery routine which consisted of walking, deep breathing and exercises. This he accomplished successfully without the infections which plagued other heart patients. He was discharged after eight days. Then began three months of hard work to restore his body to the health and strength that would enable him to return to the work he enjoyed.

He found the mandatory walks he needed each day somewhat boring until I reminded him of the many people who would be envious of this ability. This was compensated for when we drove to our favourite local areas. We both loved the sound of the ocean, the expanse of sky and the soaring flight of the eagles we were occasionally treated to. I was continually grateful.

The Gift

Each gift the Universe bestows upon us is precious beyond measure.

Then one day it happened. I found I could see internal organs, arteries, skeletal structure and brain composition in other people. I was both shocked and elated. Was this the gift I had been promised? Not wanting to be intrusive, I instinctively only practised this newly given gift with permission, to family and friends. My inner vision improved and refined. The ability to "see" disease and source its origin increased rapidly. I began to realise that I had needed to experience "the dark night of my soul" and rise again. This had enabled me to receive this gift and to connect with the souls I had seen in dreams and visions who were reaching out to me for help.

I began to have paranormal experiences. The first was an alien being, who appeared in our kitchen as I was preparing my lunch. I turned and there he was, large as life. In fact, larger. He was slim and bore some resemblance to a human, but with piercing eyes. His garment was a pale tan tunic and loosely fitting pants. I felt no threat from him, he was just watching me with interest, and soon disappeared from sight. The next were what I called "night visitors." I had two visits from a friend's father and two from other male spirits, the last so close to me that I recoiled, startled.

After this last one, I sent an urgent request for protection to my Guardian Angel and Spirit Guides. I knew they meant me no harm, they were caught between this world and the next and they needed help to move on. I felt they were lost souls and I was ill equipped to help their plight at that time. Following this, there were no more for a while. Until one night, my mother appeared at the foot of my bed and with a gentle smile, reassured me of my safety. My most recent visitor took my breath away with her beauty and her shining silvery gown. It was my Guardian Angel. I was ecstatic with joy and gratitude.

Throughout my recovery, although Helen had been a wonderful source of support and comfort I could feel her health declining. She was as feisty as ever, but the pain she endured from her fibromyalgia and her hip which badly needed a replacement, dragged her to the depths of depression. Added to her need for pain-killers, her love of an afternoon glass or two of wine and her concern for her beloved dog Sooty was a fear of being confined to a nursing home or care facility. She eventually confided her desire to end her life, and although initially shocked, I came to understand. Her need to continue her work in the spirit world overrode her desire to remain in this life.

A date was planned in accordance with both intuition and universal timing. I both anticipated and dreaded the day arriving, realising how much I would miss her. Her witty rapport, steadfast beliefs, and her wisdom, had sustained and supported me for more than two decades. My last words, with tears filling my eyes, were whispered to her as she lay in a coma. I knew she could hear me, and I once again felt her unconditional love flowing out to comfort me. The following weeks found me in an emotional mess, weeping at the smallest thing. But there was worse to come.

Four weeks later, Ann, my sister-in-law, unexpectedly took her own life. The shock of this tragedy filled me with renewed distress. Added to which, another close friend and colleague had received a message that she must move on and cease our daily contact and long phone conversations. Over Christmas and the New Year, I moved as if in a dream, frequently in tears over this triple parting. I felt alone as though cut off from these women I had held so dear. Although Hugh was continually supportive, comforting me during my low, almost depressive moments, I missed the closeness of my female friends.

Time passed as it does, and I began to climb out of this abyss. Appreciation and gratitude surfaced once more and I again took interest in my life path. Healing and helping those in need were and are my priority. More insights and lessons I had brought with me emerged. I instinctively knew it was the right time, orchestrated by the Universe. Now is the time that humanity is not only ready but hungry for this knowledge, such is this time of tumultuous change. Many feel they are being tossed and tangled, lost in the powerful new energies. Fear and confusion are abundant, terrorism rears its head and spills over to threaten every country. Humanity needs a life-raft of support and comparative security to survive this time, as we prepare to enter the coming Golden Age. I am told to share the knowledge I have brought into this lifetime, also the knowledge I have learned during my sojourn here.

Each morning I give gratitude for the abundance in my life – not of a financial nature, but far more valuable. For the abundance of intuition. For the gift of healing ability. For the love that surrounds me and permeates my very soul. For my loving family and friends. For my very special husband and life partner, who has been my life-spring over the years and who has brought understanding, laughter and deep, lasting love into my life.

In spite of having such a short stay in my last life, each day was filled with important information which I was to retain and carry with me into this life. Information which will ultimately help all humanity and our beautiful planet move from the present chaos into the coming Golden Age. You may be asking yourself, "what have I brought into this lifetime?", "what gifts do I have?", or "what is my life purpose." This is where intuition can help. We all have it. However, we need to develop and nurture it. Here are a few tips and techniques to help increase your intuition. You may experience some or all of these as your intuition increases:

Intuitive knowing. You inwardly know of a forthcoming event or happening.

Seeing through your third eye or your imagination, the answer to a question. It may come as words in capital letters in front of you, or maybe a scene acted out.

Feeling. Have you ever had a strong feeling not to travel on a certain route, or not to leave your home at all on a certain day? Remember, your first intuition is nearly always ninety-nine percent correct.

Hearing. You may hear a message, words of comfort, or even a way to help a friend.

Please share your intuitions, especially those which prove to be correct.

Please feel free to email at diana@beingnaturallyhealthy.com

Here are some guidelines to help you.

> Set your intuition to turn on your inner GPS each morning as you meditate.

> Journaling your "gut feelings" will help you clarify and refine your intuition at all levels.

> Prioritize your "me time" and tune into your inner voice.

> Walking or spending time in nature is a wonderful habit that can awaken all aspects of your intuition, as can watching a sunrise or a sunset.

> Receive and be inspired by all the gifts Mother Nature is offering.

Insights and lessons

Here are the lessons and insights I have been entrusted to share with everyone who is willing to listen. They are to be shared, as an ever-widening circle from a single drop of water that ripples outwards to all beings.

Unconditional love for all beings, for we are all one.

Love yourself with all your faults.

Love and nurture our beautiful planet, for it is unique and precious.

Forgive. You cannot be whole or move forward without forgiving others and forgiving yourself for the mistakes you have made.

Cultivate a spiritual practice and communicate with your Divine every day. Whether it is God, Spirit, Buddha, Shiva, Mother Earth, Mother Nature, the Sun, Moon or your Higher Self.

Do no harm, either to your fellow beings or to Mother Earth.

As you begin each day, give gratitude for all the blessings you have received. Restful sleep. Warm clothes. Good food. The gifts of speech, hearing, touch, taste, smell and intuition. Any special gifts which may be unique to you. If you are grateful for what you have, you will attract more of the same.

Spend time in nature every day, walk with bare feet whenever possible. Lie or sit on the grass or beach. Touch a tree and feel it's energy, or better still, hug a tree. Doing this is also a wonderful help for depression and low mood.

Care for and nurture your body, for it is a gift and not to be treated badly, neglected or abused.

Do not interfere in the Laws of Nature by genetically modifying her perfect design. Mankind will not thrive with foods altered in this way.

Be open to receiving miracles. They happen every day. You may be thinking, "well they don't happen to me." Here is the key to attracting miracles of any kind into your life - just ask. Believe with all your heart and inner being that your request has already been heard and granted. Then most importantly, give thanks and express love, and gratitude to the Universe. Be patient. Not all miracles happen immediately.

Dance helps to bring you into line with Mother Earth's energy and to feel one with her vibration. Ancient Indigenous people knew and understood this and by connecting with bare feet in this way they felt her energy and were rejuvenated.

Eat plenty of fresh organic vegetables, fruit, nuts, seeds, free range eggs and fish.

Drink plenty of filtered water.

Bless and give thanks for your food.

Infuse love as you prepare and cook your meals to enable your food to nourish your mind, body, and spirit.

Live in the moment. Life rushes past and it is so easy to think about the past with either regret for actions taken or words said. Even happy memories take us away from enjoying the present. Many of our thoughts, maybe fear of the future, of what may happen tomorrow, next week or next year.

Be focused on your life purpose.

Be aware of those who may be needing your help.

Be alert for messages.

Life balance. Achieve harmony in your life. Balance work, home responsibilities and leisure time. Make sure to set aside at least thirty minutes each day for "you time".

Energy healing. The Universe is energy and energy healing involves channelling this energy to help restore good health and facilitate the removal and dissipation of disease and illness. Trained healers have this ability.

Doing something you love. Whether it is walking in the fresh air (which I highly recommend), swimming, reading a good book, craft work or participating in sport, yoga, qigong or tai chi.

Be true to yourself. Speak your truth. That which you know is good information or knowledge.

Attitude is everything. Replace resentment, greed, and envy with joy and selfless love.

Delete the superior attitude of judging others, for we are all one. Everyone is on their own journey in this life. They may have encountered or are still encountering difficult life challenges.

Whatever we think, say or do, resonates throughout the Universe as ripples in water spread and multiply.

Trust. Everything happens for our highest good. This is one of life's most challenging lessons.

It takes up to twenty-four hours to dissipate negativity from your mind. Positivity will bring happiness in anticipating the best for yourself and for all humanity.

Personal change will increase planetary harmony. If you heal yourself, you will assist in healing our planet.

I believe meditation to be one of the most powerful practices for personal change at all levels of your being. It has major benefits for physical health. Here are a few:

Improved metabolism.

Help with loss and grief.

Increased ability to achieve a deep and restful sleep.

Improved brain function.

Lowering of blood pressure.

Decreased tension headaches and muscular aches.

Reduced stress.

Boosting of your immune system and even reduced ageing.

Quite an impressive list. Added to that are the mental and emotional benefits which include:

Decreased anxiety levels.

Increased intuition.

Reduced perception of any problems we may have.

Increased happiness.

Peace of mind and emotional stability.

Being in a state of serenity and of calm, enables this to be radiated out to your environment, ultimately bringing harmony to our planet.

Because we lead such busy lives, many people believe they have little or no time for meditation. Not so. Try this breath technique which takes only minutes and can be done at your desk or your lunch break or better still walking out in nature.

> Take a deep breath with your belly and as you do so visualise peace, calm, and harmony infusing your whole being. Breathe out, letting stress, frustration, and anger go with the breath.

Repeat this technique as many times as you feel you need and enjoy your new found serenity.

ℰpilogue

Embrace the future, but while doing so savour every moment of every day, for it will not come again.

As I write, sitting quietly, my mind closed to the busyness around me, I reflect on global developments of the past year. The increase in humanity's distress and that of Mother Earth. The increase in unspeakable acts of terror across the planet and the dramatic climactic events reflecting Mother Earth's anger. How can we help in reversing this overwhelming evil, pollution, crime, depression, and desperation that is engulfing mankind? Here are two simple yet powerful ways to manifest change, which are achievable either singly, or for increased impact, with a group.

> Many people are familiar with Dr. Masaru Emoto's experiments with water, whereby he unveiled proof that our emotions and thoughts affect the structure of water, especially when sourced from pristine springs. The water infused with happy thoughts such as love, peace or harmony, caused it to form beautiful, symmetrical and often intricate snow flake-like images. Whereas emotions such as anger or hate brought about ugly, shapeless images. Bearing in mind our bodies are composed of approximately eighty percent water and the earth fifty percent, infusing your water with love before consuming it will assist in healing your body, as well as our precious planet.

> This has been demonstrated in another experiment known as "The Maharishi Effect", whereby a critical mass of one percent of a city's population meditates together. With Transcendental Meditation or calming of the mind in consciousness, the energy generated transforms the community to one of peace and increased contentment. This meditation is so powerful it has been proven to reduce crime by up to eighteen percent and pollution and terrorism by a similar percentage in any given city. On a wider perspective, if enough people were to participate, we could embody worldwide peace, harmony, and love. An awesome concept indeed. A daily meditative practice can literally change your health and wellbeing and assist with planetary healing.

What lessons have I learned in this life, and in fact am still learning? One of my greatest and most difficult lessons has been to never give up once I have set a goal, no matter how difficult it is to achieve. Some of my life's goals have appeared as mountains, impossible for me to climb, but the more steps I have taken, the more tools and assistance I have received from friends, family and most of all, the Universe. That mountain was reduced to an insignificant bump on my path.

The second is to trust. Trust my innermost feelings and my intuition. Trust that all that has happened has ultimately been for my highest good. Many times I have asked, "why has this happened to me?" Not from despair, but "what has this been sent to teach me?" This was followed with further understanding of the Laws of the Universe and how, why and where they fit into the Divine Plan.

My mistakes, of which there are more than a few, have been my teacher. Learning to love myself has been an uphill struggle. Until, at the top of the mountain, again in the light, I saw forgiveness streaming into my soul and I was born anew. Some Universal secrets have been revealed to me in this life, but they will remain a secret until humankind is ready to accept these truths.

I have been given the secrets to wellness and vibrant health at any age. I have a free e-book in which I have shared some of these secrets. It is available on my website www.beingnaturallyhealthy.com. I have learned a life without a spiritual practice such as meditation, yoga, qi-gong and prayer, is an incomplete life.

Life is filled with change. However, I have found acceptance to change a challenge at times. I consider adapting to change to be an important lesson. I have seen many people find it difficult to work towards its total integration into their lives.

Mountaintop meditation

Take two or three deep breaths. As you breathe in, bring in peace and serenity, and as you breathe out, let go of stress and anxiety. Place it into a balloon and watch it float away.

Close your eyes and gently relax your mind. Let go of your thoughts. Watch them disappear into the atmosphere. Relax your arms, your legs, and your whole body. Now imagine you are sitting on the top of a mountain, looking out at the sun as it slowly rises above the horizon in a golden mystical ball of light. Feel the gentle warmth of its rays, bringing the promise of new beginnings and opportunities into your life. Behind you is the past. Spend a few moments reviewing it. Now let it go, for it has no relevance for you in this new beginning.

Now focus on the present. Your blessings so freely given by the Universe. The unconditional love. The courage. The strength you are given each day. Project gratitude and appreciation. Greet this dawn with positivity and joy. Sit peacefully on your mountain and take a few minutes to contemplate and focus on these blessings. Now spread love and gratitude into the Universe and around our beautiful planet. Know that guidance will be given when you need it, all you have to do is ask. Believe in miracles for they will appear.

Now, imagine pure white light surrounding you. Feel its warmth, its protection and the unconditional love it imparts. Pull this light down through your crown chakra, feel it slowly filling your body, mind, and spirit with joy and peace. Remain with this sacred energy for a while, then when you are ready, slowly return from this place. Move your arms and legs and stretch your whole body before slowly opening your eyes. Rest for a while before resuming your daily tasks.

$\mathcal{B}$iography

Born in the United Kingdom, Diana now lives in Sydney, Australia. She is passionate about the healing power of nature and the body's ability to heal itself. Diana gained a Diploma of Horticulture in her late teens. Working closely with the Earth's energies she gained an insight into the powers of Mother Earth and Universal Healing.

Diana has been gifted with intuition and the ability to "see" any malfunction of internal organs, find the origin of disease, pain, and illness and treat them at their source.

This is Diana's first book. She is also featured in *Women of the Wise Earth* and is a co-author of *The Change* book series.

Diana is a certified 21st Century Energy Practitioner, Medical Intuitive, and Wellness Life Coach.

Diana@beingnaturallyhealthy.com
www.beingnaturallyhealthy.com

Testimonials

"Diana is a beautiful person with an amazing gift to see inside the human body and heal. She has treated all our family with incredible results. In particular, Diana has worked extensively on our 2-year-old's health problems and the recovery has been nothing short of a miracle. We have recommended Diana to friends and family who also echo our thoughts that Diana is absolutely "the real deal". Her empathetic and kind nature, coupled with her incredible ability, make her an outstanding medical intuitive healer." Kate F.

"Diana is the REAL DEAL and, as an added bonus, her presence and energy is like talking to an Angel. I've worked with many healers and healing systems so I feel qualified to offer this recommendation. After our first session, I broke down in tears. Mostly from her love and support BUT, because I finally felt 'heard'. She saw me – ALL of me – confirmed what I knew, could literally see every problem area, down to vertebra (without prior knowledge) and she has the most amazing ability to hold a space of unconditional love and a knowing that all will be well. I cannot recommend her enough. Part of Diana's work is to uncover and clear self-sabotage mental programs – SHE IS AMAZING AT THIS, I love her and I know you will too." Katherine S. K.

Printed in the United States
By Bookmasters